REGIONAL TRAMWAYS

MIDLANDS & SOUTHERN ENGLAND

REGIONAL TRAMWAYS

MIDLANDS & SOUTHERN ENGLAND

PETER WALLER

PEN & SWORD
TRANSPORT

AN IMPRINT OF PEN & SWORD BOOKS LTD.
YORKSHIRE – PHILADELPHIA

Regional Tramways: Midlands and Southern England

First published in Great Britain in 2018 by
Pen & Sword Transport
An imprint of Pen & Sword Books Ltd
Yorkshire - Philadelphia

ISBN 978 1 47387 114 4

Typeset in 11/13 Palatino by Aura Technology and Software services, India

Printed and bound in India by Replika Press Pvt. Ltd.

Pen & Sword Books Ltd incorporates the Imprints of Pen & Sword Books Archaeology, Atlas, Aviation, Battleground, Discovery, Family History, History, Maritime, Military, Naval, Politics, Railways, Select, Transport, True Crime, Fiction, Frontline Books, Leo Cooper, Praetorian Press, Seaforth Publishing, Wharncliffe and White Owl.

For a complete list of Pen & Sword titles please contact

PEN & SWORD BOOKS LIMITED
47 Church Street, Barnsley, South Yorkshire, S70 2AS, England
E-mail: enquiries@pen-and-sword.co.uk
Website: www.pen-and-sword.co.uk

or

PEN AND SWORD BOOKS
1950 Lawrence Rd, Havertown, PA 19083, USA
E-mail: Uspen-and-sword@casematepublishers.com
Website: www.penandswordbooks.com

CONTENTS

ABBREVIATIONS

BEC	British Electric Car Co Ltd, Trafford Park, Manchester
BET	British Electric Traction
BR	British Railways
EMB	Electro-Mechanical Brake Co Ltd
DMU	Diesel multiple unit
ERTCW	Electric Railway & Tramway Carriage Works
GWR	Great Western Railway
L&CBER	Llandudno & Colwyn Bay Electric Railway
LMS	London, Midland & Scottish Railway
LNER	London & North Eastern Railway
LNWR	London & North Western Railway
LRTL	Light Railway Transport League
M&G	Mountain & Gibson Truck & Engineering Co Ltd
M&T	Maley & Taunton
Milnes	G. F. Milnes & Co, Birkenhead, and later Hadley, in Shropshire
NTM	National Tramway Museum
SER	South Eastern Railway
PAYE	Pay as you enter
TUCC	Transport Users Consultative Committee
UDC	Urban District Council
UEC	United Electric Car Co Ltd, Preston

KEY TO MAPS

Passenger lines
Lines closed before 1 January 1945
Non-passenger lines
Lines of neighbouring operators – open at 1 January 1945
Lines of neighbouring operators – closed at 1 January 1945
Passenger lines built opened after 1 January 1945
Lines under construction at 1 January 1945 – never completed

PREFACE

This is the fifth in a series that is intended, ultimately, to cover all the tramways of the British Isles. Its focus is primarily on those tramway systems in the Midlands, Southern and Eastern England. However, it also provides an overview of tramway development from the horse-tram era onwards. Following the introduction, there are individual chapters dealing with each of the first-generation tramways that survived into 1945, with a map that shows the system as it existed at 1 January 1945 and a fleet list of all the trams operated after that date. The volume also includes two second generation tramways — Midland Metro and Nottingham Express Transit.

The majority of illustrations in the book are drawn from the collection of Online Transport Archive; in particular, I'd like to express my gratitude to the late Arthur Brookes, Barry Cross, Peter Davey, the late W.S. Eades, the late R.W.A. Jones, the late F.K. Farrell, the late F.N.T. Lloyd-Jones, John Meredith, the late R.

Stephens, the late Phil Tatt, the late F.E.J. Ward, the late P.N. Williams and Ian L. Wright — all of whose negatives or collections are now in the care of OTA (Online Transport Archive) — and the National Tramway Museum in whose care the collections of the late R.B. Parr and the late W.A. Camwell now reside. Martin Jenkins has been a great help in trying to track down certain images and providing comment. Every effort has been made to try and ensure complete accuracy; unfortunately, the records available are not always consistent and, with the passage of time, the number of those with detailed knowledge is gradually declining. Likewise, every effort has been made to ensure the correct attribution of photographs. It goes without saying that any errors of fact or attribution are the author's and any corrections should be forwarded on to him care of the publishers.

Peter Waller,
Shrewsbury,
August 2017

INTRODUCTION

It was not until the Tramways Act of 1870 that a legal framework existed to permit the construction of street tramways. The American entrepreneur George Francis Train discovered this during the early 1860s when he endeavoured to build a number of street tramways in England. The act authorised local authorities to grant the rights to operate tramways within the local area to companies for a period of 21 years; construction of the tramway could either be undertaken by the authority and leased to the operator or by the operator itself. The act also imposed a duty upon the operator to maintain the strip of road 18in either side of the outer running rails; in many ways, this was the Achilles' heel of the act: at a time when roads were generally badly maintained — if they were maintained at all — the creation of this well-managed strip in the middle meant that it became available to all road users and the tram increasingly became perceived as a cause of delays to other road users as a consequence. At the end of the twenty-one-year lease, or periodically thereafter, the local authority was entitled to purchase the assets of the company at a written-down value. This was a further weakness in the act in that it dissuaded the leaseholders from investing further in the business as the potential selling price would not reflect the investment undertaken. The 1870 act was subsequently amended, most notably with the Light Railways Act of 1896, but represented the basis upon which most tramways were built.

The Portsmouth Street Tramways Co was formed from lines constructed by four different companies; it was to pass to corporation operation on 1 January 1901. *Barry Cross Collection/ Online Transport Archive*

The first tramway to open in the areas covered by this volume predated the 1870 Act; this was the two-mile route of the Landport & Southsea Tramways Co, which commenced operation on 15 May 1865. This company, which obtained a private act in 1863, operated between the station and Southsea Pier. This was followed on 11 September 1874 by the line from Floating Bridge to North End, which was operated by the Portsmouth Street Tramways Co, and on 18 March 1878 by a third operator, the General Tramways Co of Portsmouth Ltd. These three companies all became subsidiaries of the Portsmouth Street Tramways Co, a subsidiary of the Provincial Tramways Co, in August 1883. A fourth horse operator — the Portsmouth (Borough)

Kingston, Fratton & Southsea Co — commenced operation on 18 March 1878 and passed to the Portsmouth Street Tramways Co in 1892. At its maximum extent, the Portsmouth Street Tramways Co operated 65 trams over a network of 12 route miles. Operation passed to the corporation on 1 January 1901 and the last horse trams operated in May 1903.

The first horse trams to operate in Plymouth were the standard gauge cars of the Plymouth, Stonehouse & Devonport Tramways Co that commenced operation on 18 March 1872 on a route from Millbay to Market Street along Union Street — a distance of just under half-a-mile. Horse operation ceased in 1901 when the line was regauged to 3ft 6in and extended for electric operation.

One of the Plymouth, Stonehouse & Devonport's fleet of 12 horse trams heads westwards at the Battery Street loop in 1900. The Grand theatre on the left had opened the previous year. *Barry Cross Collection/ Online Transport Archive*

Although the next trams in Plymouth were steam operated, these were short-lived and had ceased operation by the end of 1885. The company's 3ft 6in route — from Millbay to Mannamead — was taken over by a new company, the Plymouth Tramways Co, which commenced horse operation in 1890. It was acquired by the corporation two years later and extended, with the horse network reaching a maximum extent of about 6½ route miles. The corporation started to electrify the system in 1899 and the last horse trams operated on 22 June 1907.

The first horse trams in Birmingham — courtesy of the Birmingham & District Tramways Co Ltd — commenced operation on 11 September 1873 from the borough boundary at Hockley Brook through to the town centre at the future Colmore Row (known at the time as Monmouth Street); at Hockley Brook it linked with the existing company route to Hill Top via Dudley Port, which had opened on 20 May 1872. The first routes were constructed to standard gauge as was a line from Monmouth Street to Bournbrook; this opened on 17 June 1876 and was operated by the Birmingham Tramways & Omnibus Co (which had taken over the earlier Birmingham & District on 24 May 1876). This company passed to the Birmingham Central Tramway Co — which had begun horse operation on a 3ft 6in route to Nechells Park Road on 25 November 1884 — in January 1886 and to the City of

At its maximum extent, Plymouth Corporation employed 54 horse trams; this is No 2 pictured at St Jude's Church. *Barry Cross Collection/Online Transport Archive*

The first trams in Birmingham were standard gauge horse trams operated by the Birmingham & District Tramways Co Ltd in 1873. *W. S. Eades Collection/Online Transport Archive*

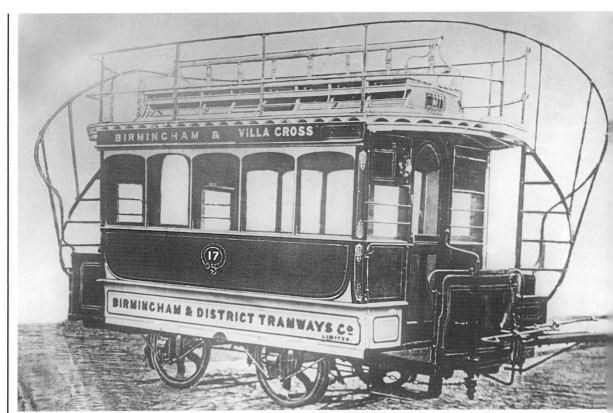

The last horse tram operated by the City of Birmingham Tramways Co Ltd is pictured at Nechells on 30 September 1906. *Barry Cross Collection/Online Transport Archive*

Birmingham Tramways Co a decade later. The routes opened in Birmingham in 1873 and 1876 were built to standard gauge; with the development of the steam tram network operated by the Birmingham & Suburban Tramways Co Ltd from 1881 onwards all new routes were constructed to 3ft 6in. The last horse trams operated in Birmingham on 30 September 1906.

Horse tram operation commenced in Leicester, following the Leicester Tramways Order of 1873, on 24 December 1874. The standard gauge route operated by the Leicester Tramways Co linked the Clock Tower to Belgrave. Two further routes were added in 1875 — east along Humberstone Road and south-east along London Road — with further extensions following later in the decade. The company's assets were acquired by the corporation on 1 July 1901; at that date, the fleet comprised 39 horse trams plus 30 horse buses. Following electrification, the last horse trams operated on 31 October 1904.

Following powers obtained in 1871, the East Suffolk Tramway Co constructed a standard gauge tramway from Yarmouth Southtown station to Gorleston; services commenced on 1 April 1875. Three years later, the Yarmouth & Gorleston Tramways Co Ltd was established to take over the existing tramway. The new owner reconstructed the line to 3ft 6in gauge in 1882 and opened three short extensions — in 1884, 1886 and 1898 — that took the route to just over two miles in length. The company was acquired by BET in 1900, creating a new subsidiary — the Great Yarmouth & District Tramways Co Ltd — for the purpose. However, the corporation decided upon municipal operation; following the corporation's take-over, the last horse trams operated on the route to Gorleston on 4 July 1905.

Established in 1874, the Bristol Tramways Co Ltd introduced standard gauge horse trams to the city on 9 August 1875. The first route was that to Redland

Horse trams — such as No 2 seen here — operated in Leicester courtesy of the Leicester Tramways Co from 24 December 1874. Following the corporation take-over, the last horse trams operated in October 1904. *Barry Cross Collection/ Online Transport Archive*

A horse tram from the Yarmouth & Gorleston Tramways Co is pictured in Gorleston's High Street. The route was operated by horse trams for some 30 years. *Barry Cross Collection/Online Transport Archive*

Horse trams first operated in Bristol in 1875, but this view must post-date 1887 as it was in October that year that the Bristol Tramways & Carriage Co Ltd was established following a merger between two earlier operators. *Barry Cross Collection/Online Transport Archive*

GORLESTON — High Street

and the network expanded to some 20 route miles. The company was renamed the Bristol Tramways & Carriage Co Ltd on 1 October 1887 following a merger with the Bristol Carriage Co Ltd. Following the introduction of electric trams in 1895, the final horse trams operated in 1900.

The Wantage Tramway, linking Wantage Road station on the Great Western main line between Swindon and Didcot and Wantage, was authorised in 1873. The 2½-mile long standard gauge line opened to freight traffic on 1 October 1875 and to passenger traffic on the 10th. Initially, passenger traffic was horse-powered but an Act of 27 June 1876, confirming a provisional order made in 1870, permitted the use of steam although limited horse operation continued into the 1880s. Steam operation commenced on 1 August 1876;

passenger services were withdrawn on 31 July 1925, with freight traffic surviving until 22 December 1945.

Authorised the previous year, standard gauge horse trams commenced operation in Wolverhampton courtesy of the Wolverhampton Tramways Co on 1 May 1878. Eventually three routes — totalling just over 8½ route miles — were operated. In 1881, the company briefly experimented with steam operation, using an engine acquired from the Hughes's Locomotive & Tramway Engine Works of Loughborough. Operation was transferred to Wolverhampton Corporation on 1 May 1900 with horse operation ceasing in 1903. One of the company's trams — No 23 — was eventually rescued for preservation in 1973; it is currently displayed in a restored condition at the Black Country Museum.

Although initial services on the Wantage Tramway were horse-operated, less than a year after the line opened steam – in the form of this experimental steam-powered tramcar designed by John Grantham – was introduced. More conventional steam tram engines were acquired from late 1876 onwards and horse operation ceased during the 1880s. *Barry Cross Collection/Online Transport Archive*

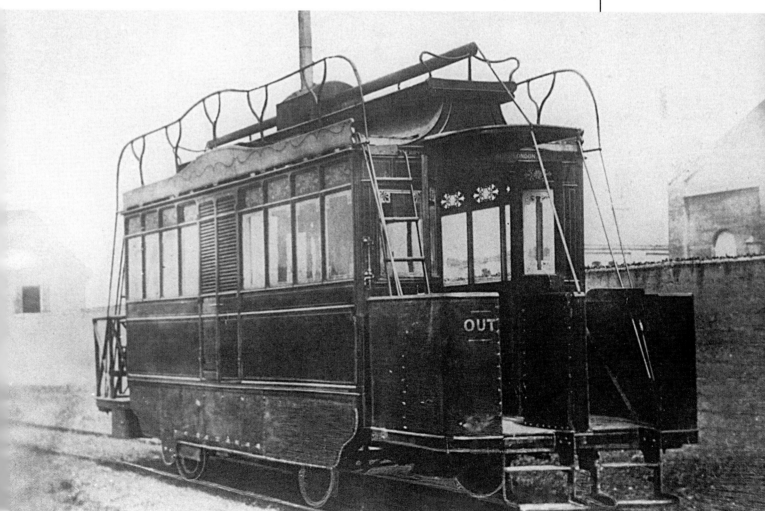

Nottingham &
District No 7 is seen in service during 1895; the majority of the company's fleet was initially single-deck, supplied by either Starbuck of Birkenhead or John Stevenson & Co of New York, but these were subsequently replaced by double-deck trams supplied by Milnes or Brush. *Barry Cross Collection/Online Transport Archive*

Southampton Tramways Co No 19 was one of 11 supplied by Starbuck between 1879 and 1882. In all the company employed 37 trams during its 20-year existence. *Barry Cross Collection/Online Transport Archive*

Although there were proposals earlier in the decade, it was not until 17 September 1878 that the first section of the standard gauge network of the Nottingham & District Tramways Co Ltd officially opened. With an ultimate length of 6¼ route miles, three routes were operated. Although there were proposals for further extensions, these were never completed and, following purchase, the corporation acquired the operation on 18 October 1897. The last horse trams operated on 30 April 1902.

The Southampton Tramways Co introduced horse trams to the town on 5 May 1879. The standard gauge system eventually extended over almost five route miles, with services operating to the Docks via Holy Rood, to Portswood and to Shirley. In all, the company operated 37 trams and its assets were taken over by Southampton Corporation on 1 July 1898 with the final horse trams operated on 2 August 1901.

Horse operation in Reading commenced in May 1879 over a route linking Oxford Road, near Reading West railway station, with Cemetery Junction via the town centre. Operated by the Reading Tramways Co, the route was taken over by the corporation on 31 October 1901. The new owners sought to extend the network; initially, horse trams operated over these new routes pending the completion of electrification. Horse tram operation finally ceased on 21 July 1903 prior to the introduction of replacement electric trams over the original route.

Also commencing operation in May 1879, on the 26th of the month, were the horse trams operated by the Gloucester Tramways Co. Six short radiating routes were operated, totalling just under 3½ route

At its peak, the Reading Tramways Co used 13 horse trams; one of these is pictured in Broad Street. Originally the fleet was entirely single-deck, but by the cessation of company ownership all were double-deckers. *Barry Cross Collection/Online Transport Archive*

At its peak the Gloucester Tramways Co employed a fleet of 14 single-deck trams constructed by Bristol, Brush, the locally based Gloucester Railway Carriage & Wagon Co Ltd and Starbuck. *Barry Cross Collection/Online Transport Archive*

miles, with a fleet of fourteen 4ft 0in gauge trams. The corporation took over on 1 January 1903 with a view to electrifying the network and the last horse trams in the city operated on 17 March 1904.

The Derby Tramways Co Ltd introduced 4ft 0in gauge horse trams to Derby on 6 March 1880 with a route linking the Market Place with the Midland Railway station. Further routes followed with the

The Derby Tramways Co operated horse trams in Derby between 1880 and the corporation take-over in 1899. *Barry Cross Collection/ Online Transport Archive*

Following its take over in 1899, Derby Corporation operated the horse-tram network whilst it was electrified; the last horse trams operated on 1 June 1907. *Barry Cross Collection/Online Transport Archive*

system extending over some 4¾ route miles at its maximum extent. In all, some 23 horse trams were operated with routes radiating from the centre over the Ashbourne, London, Normanton and Osmaston roads.

The corporation took over on 1 November 1899 and, following electrification, the last horse trams operated on 1 June 1907.

Horse tram operation commenced in Ipswich on 13 October 1880 over a route

The Ipswich Tramway Co employed nine horse trams, of which six — Nos 4 to 9 — were double-deck, being new in 1882 and 1884. One of these is illustrated here; the fleet livery was maroon and cream. *Barry Cross Collection/Online Transport Archive*

Cambridge Street
Tramways Co No 5
is pictured outside
the Senate House
during a university
procession. This
was one of two
trams — the other
being No 6 — that
had an internal
partition to create
a space capable of
accommodating
students' luggage for
journeys to and from
the railway station.
This was little used
and the partitions
were removed in
1892. *Barry Cross
Collection/Online
Transport Archive*

linking the Cornhill in the town centre
with the railway station plus a branch to
Brooks Hall via Portman Road. Operation
passed to the Ipswich Tramway Co in
1881, under whose control a number of
extensions were constructed. Eventually,
the 4ft 0in system extended to 4¼ route
miles with the final extension, from
Cornhill to Derby Road station, being
completed in 1884. The assets of the
company were acquired by the corporation
on 1 November 1901 and the final horse
trams operated on 6 June 1903.

From 28 October 1880, the Cambridge
Street Tramways introduced 4ft 0in horse
trams to the university city. The system
eventually comprised two routes — from
the railway station to Christ's College
and from Newmarket Road to the Senate
House — and a total of eight trams were
operated over just over 2½ route miles.
Although there were proposals in the late

1890s from BET to electrify and extend the
system, these came to nothing and, with
the introduction of bus competition in 1905
and again in 1907, the economics of the
system declined and the last horse trams
operated on 18 February 1914. One of the
fleet, No 7 – built originally in 1880 and
acquired by the company in 1894 – was
secured for preservation in 1993 and is
now undergoing restoration at the Ipswich
Transport Museum.

The Bath Tramways Co introduced
4ft 0in gauge horse trams to the city on
24 December 1880 on a route from the
GWR station to Grosvenor College. The
route extended over about 1¾ miles but
was not a financial success and, on 26
May 1884, the operator was taken over by
the Patent Cable Tramways Corporation;
this too was to fail, being taken over
by Dick, Kerr & Co on 11 August 1888.
A further change of ownership occurred on

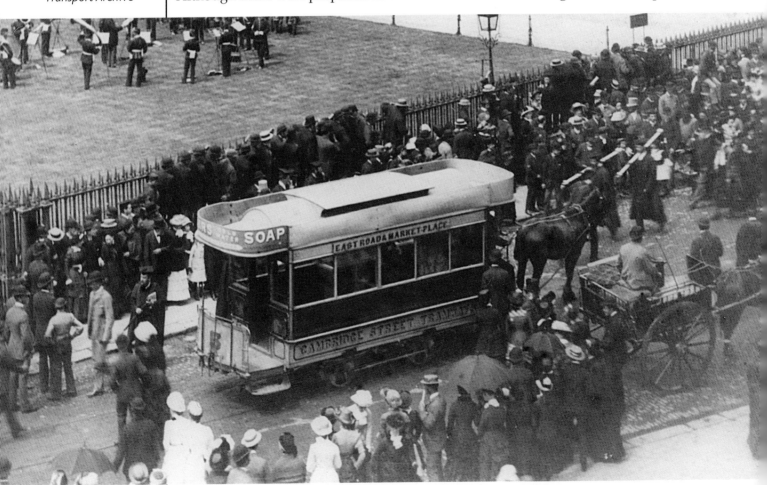

1 April 1889 when the tramway passed to the Bath Road Car & Tramways Co. Horse operation ceased on 25 July 1902 when the assets were taken over by the corporation pending the route's electrification.

Established in 1880, the Northampton Street Tramways Co commenced horse tram operation in the town on 4 June 1881. The initial route linked the town centre to the Kingley Park Hotel along the Kettering Road. The system was extended through until 18 May 1893 when the line along Wellingborough Road towards Weston Favell was opened. The corporation took over the 3ft 6in system on 21 October 1901 and the final horse trams operated on 18 August 1904.

Opened in 1881, the Great Grimsby Street Tramways Co provided a standard gauge link initially from Grimsby town centre to the boundary between Grimsby and Cleethorpes. It was extended twice — in 1887 and 1898 — to reach the seafront in Cleethorpes. There was also a one-mile branch in Grimsby along Freeman Street. Following reconstruction, the network was electrified and the final horse trams operated in 1901.

The standard gauge horse trams of the Leamington & Warwick Tramways & Omnibus Co commenced operation on 21 November 1881. In all, nine trams were operated over the three-mile route. The company was acquired by BET in 1900 and powers to electrify the line were obtained the following year. The last horse trams operated on 15 March 1905. Of the fleet, two cars survive; No 1 is in an unrestored condition at the NTM whilst No 8 is under restoration at Beamish (where it will emerge in the guise of a Newcastle & Gosforth car).

Like its academic rival in Cambridgeshire, the city of Oxford only

Northampton Street Tramways Co No 3 pictured at the St James' Road terminus; this view records the tram as it was rebuilt in 1886. It had originally been built by the Birmingham Carriage & Wagon Co in 1881. *Barry Cross Collection/Online Transport Archive*

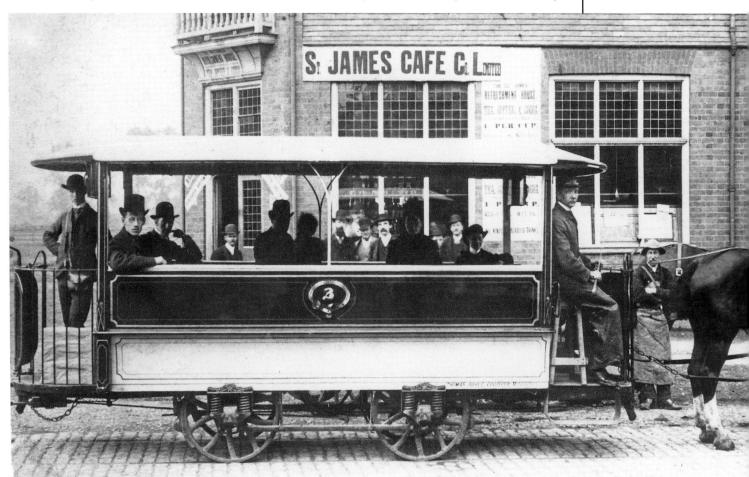

The Great Grimsby Street Tramways Co, a subsidiary of the Provincial Tramways Co, operated horse trams from 1881 until the services were electrified 20 years later. *Barry Cross Collection/Online Transport Archive*

Leamington & Warwick No 7 was one of two acquired from the Metropolitan Railway Carriage & Wagon Co in 1882; in all the company employed nine horse trams. *Barry Cross Collection/Online Transport Archive*

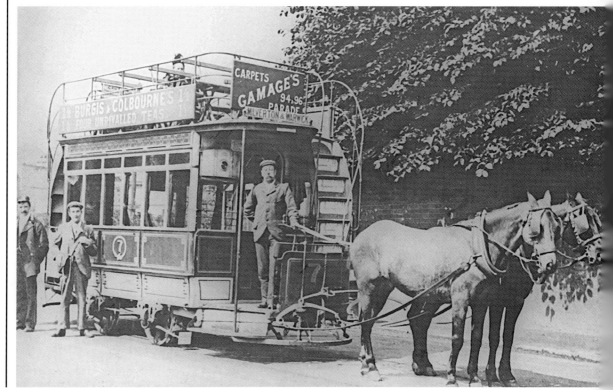

ever possessed a horse tramway. The first of the City of Oxford Tramways' 4ft 0in trams operated, on a route from the GWR's railway station to Cowley Road via Carfax, on 1 December 1881. Extensions up the Banbury Road (on 28 January 1882), to Kingston Road (on 15 July 1884) and to New Hinksey (on 15 March 1887) followed. The final extension saw the Banbury Road route extended to Summertown on 5 November 1898. The corporation took over in 1906 with a view to electrification under the auspices of the City of Oxford Electric Tramways Co, which acquired the lease the following year. Plans for electrification could not be agreed and the horse trams soldiered on until being replaced by buses on 7 August 1914.

During its 21-year life, the horse tram network in Worcester had three owners. The first, under whose auspices the 3ft 0in gauge system opened in 1881, was the Tramways Trust Co; however, this company failed and was liquidated on

12 December 1885. Its network extended over 3½ route miles. The second operator was the City of Worcester Tramways Co, which acquired the lease in 1889; again, this failed, and the company was wound up on 3 April 1894. Its assets — including nine horse trams — were acquired by the Worcester Tramways Co the same year. This new company was taken over by BET in 1898 with a view to electrification. The last horse trams operated on 25 June 1903.

Horse trams commenced operation in Exeter, courtesy of the Exeter Tramway Co, on 6 April 1882. The 3ft 6in gauge network had services to St David's station and along the Heavitree and Pinhoe roads. Unfortunately, the company was unable to operate along Queen Street and High Street, which affected its viability, with the result that it was soon in financial difficulties. The company was eventually wound up in August 1889 although a new operator took over three years later. The following year the

Pictured in 1913 towards the end of its life — note the adjacent Daimler bus; a number of these were acquired to replace the trams — is one of the City of Oxford District Tramways fleet. At its maximum, the fleet numbered 20 horse trams. *Barry Cross Collection/ Online Transport Archive*

Worcester Tramways Co No 3; this was one of six double-deck trams supplied by the Falcon Engine & Car Works (of Loughborough) in 1884 to the system's original operator. *Barry Cross Collection/Online Transport Archive*

service to St David's was abandoned. The corporation took over in 1904 with a view to electrification and the final horse trams operated on 4 April 1905.

The Lincoln Tramways Co introduced standard gauge horse trams to the city on 8 September 1882. One route — about 1¾ miles in length — operated

The Exeter Tramways Co operated three short horse tram routes until the corporation took over with the intention of electrifying the services. This tram was one of those used on the service along Heavitree Road. *Barry Cross Collection/Online Transport Archive*

from Bracebridge to St Benedict's Square; although there were plans for extensions, these came to nothing. In all, ten trams were operated with the corporation taking over in July 1904. The last horse trams operated on 22 July 1905 pending electrification.

The Chesterfield & District Tramways Co, succeeded by the Chesterfield Tramways Co in December 1886, introduced standard gauge horse trams to a 1¼-mile route from the town centre west to Bampton on 8 November 1882. In all, ten trams were operated with the last ones in service appearing, following the takeover by Chesterfield Corporation and electrification, in November 1904. One of the Milnes-built horse trams, No 8 of 1899, was rescued for preservation and, following restoration, formed part of the BTC collection. It is now part of the NTM collection.

Commencing on 15 June 1883, the Gravesend, Rosherville & Northfleet Tramways operated a single 3ft 6in gauge line between Gravesend and Northfleet. In March 1889, an extension from Northfleet to Huggins College was opened; authorised in 1884, this section was constructed by the Swiss Electrical Traction Co to demonstrate electric trams powered via a conduit. This experiment lasted through to November 1890; thereafter the entire route was horse operated. In 1901, the company was acquired by the Gravesend & Northfleet Tramways, a subsidiary of BET, with the last horse trams operating on 30 June 1901 to enable work to commence on the line's regauging and electrification.

To the west of Brighton, the Brighton District Tramways Co was authorised to construct a 3ft 6in tramway from just west of Shoreham station to the Hove

In all the Lincoln Tramways Co operated ten trams; No 3 was a 16-seat single-deck tram supplied by Ashburys in 1883. *Barry Cross Collection/Online Transport Archive*

Built by Milnes of Birkenhead, Chesterfield No 8 was new in 1899. Destined for a relatively short life — it was withdrawn in 1904 with the line's electrification — the body was rescued by the corporation and restored. Owned by the British Transport Commission from 1956, it was transferred to the tramway museum at Crich and ownership was formally passed to the NTM in September 2016. *Barry Cross Collection/Online Transport Archive*

From March 1889 to November 1890, part of the Gravesend, Rosherville & Northfleet Tramways was operated by electric trams via a conduit; two Brush-built trams were supplied for the experimental service. *Barry Cross Collection/Online Transport Archive*

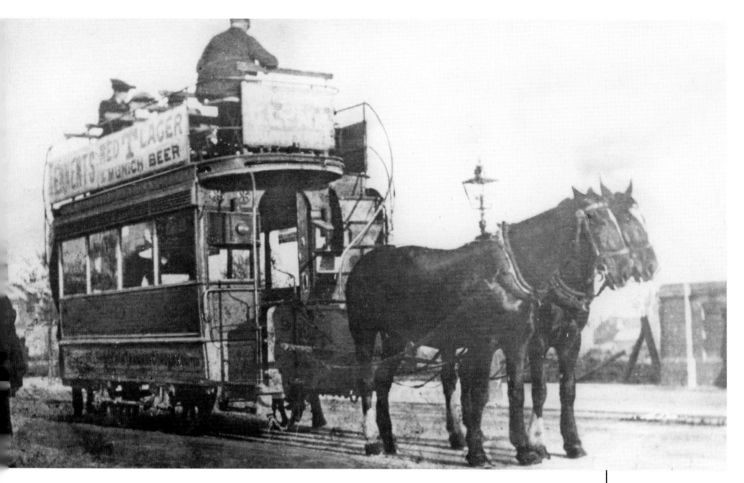

boundary. Opening on 3 July 1884, the bulk of the route — just over four miles — was steam operated, but the half-mile section west of Shoreham station was horse operated; this section, however, was to be short-lived and soon abandoned. Steam operation on the remainder of the route was also soon to disappear, being supplemented by horse operation in 1885 and completely abandoned in 1888 when a new operator — the Brighton & District Tramway Co Ltd — took over from the earlier company, which had failed. The new company was also to fail — in May 1889 — being replaced six months later by the Brighton & Shoreham Tramways Co Ltd. In 1898, the company was acquired by BET with a view to extending and electrifying the route; however, opposition from Hove Corporation was one factor in BET's failure to get authorisation for its complete scheme. Services largely ceased in October 1912,

although limited operation survived through until 6 June 1913.

The only horse tramway in southern Kent was operated by the Folkestone, Hythe & Sandgate Tramways. The line was backed by the South Eastern Railway with initial services operating from Sandgate School to the Seabrook Hotel commencing on 18 May 1881. The line was extended to Hythe on 6 June 1882, making the line just over 3¼ miles in length. Ownership was transferred from the SER — by now the South Eastern & Chatham Railway — to the Folkestone, Hythe & Sandgate Tramways Co in 1906. As a result of the First World War, services were suspended on 7 August 1914; summer-only services resumed after the war in 1919, but these were short-lived and the final trams operated on 30 September 1921. In all, five trams were operated.

Following an order made in 1880, standard gauge horse trams commenced

The Brighton & Shoreham Tramways Co Ltd was the third operator of the line; acquired by BET in 1898, the line was to be horse operated through to final closure on 6 June 1913. *Barry Cross Collection/Online Transport Archive*

In all the Folkestone, Hythe & Sandgate Tramway employed five trams; No 5, seen here at Hythe, was constructed by the South Eastern Railway at Ashford Works in 1897. It is pictured in the livery of the successor South Eastern & Chatham Railway. *Barry Cross Collection/Online Transport Archive*

operation between Dudley and Wolverhampton courtesy of the Dudley, Sedgeley & Wolverhampton Tramways Co Ltd on 7 May 1883. However, the service was not a success, largely as a result of the gradients encountered, and the horse trams ceased operating on 8 November 1885 to permit conversion of the route to steam operation.

In the early twentieth century, speculators, including a Frederick Hester, saw Canvey Island as a potentially significant holiday resort. Hester conceived the idea of a railway to improve communications. The line was built during 1901 and 1902 in the guise of a horse-operated monorail. Although Hester had grandiose plans, little was achieved, but a section did carry passengers briefly during 1902. The line's fate was sealed when Hester lost interest in the development of the island and left. There were plans for a 3ft 6in tramway along the same route in 1904; work started and trams ordered,

but flooding resulted in the failure of the project.

Proposals for a horse tramway in Aldershot were first made in the early 1860s, but it was not until the incorporation of the Aldershot & Farnborough Tramways Co following an Act of 16 August 1878 that real progress was made. The standard gauge line — which extended for about 2½ miles — was inspected on 15 August 1881 by the Board of Trade but the exact date of opening is uncertain. The company reported income of £246 and expenditure of £835 for the year to 30 June 1883, with the use of two trams and thirteen horses. Although listed by the Board of Trade between 1884 and 1887, no returns were made and the company disappeared completely in 1888. Whilst the exact date of closure is unknown, it seems likely that the tramway operated for barely a year. This was not quite the end of the tramway story in the area; in the early twentieth century, proposals for an electric tramway

were put forward; although some limited construction was undertaken, it was never completed or opened.

The Nottingham & District Tramways Co Ltd tested an experimental steam tram, supplied by Hughes & Co of Loughborough, on 7 May 1880; the same year a self-propelled tram, powered by steam and built by Manlove, Alliott & Co Ltd, was also tested (this eventually passed to the Dublin & Lucan line in Ireland). In late 1882, the company was authorised to use a steam tram engine on the Basford route for 12 months; the authorisation was renewed in April 1884 for a further 12 months. A single Wilkinson-built engine was acquired; initially this hauled a horse tram but a new trailer (No 29) — supplied by Starbuck — was acquired in 1885. The steam service was to survive until 1889

after which No 29 was modified to operate as a horse tram.

Steam trams were to be operated for a brief twelve-month period by the Bristol Tramways Co Ltd during 1880 and 1881 on the Horfield route. Elsewhere, the company persisted with the operation of horse trams, despite the additional costs incurred in the use of trace horses to cope with the gradients.

Another of the few railway-owned tramways in Great Britain was the Wolverton & Stony Stratford in Buckinghamshire. This was originally incorporated as the Wolverton & Stony Stratford Tramways Co Ltd on 4 November 1882. The 2¾-mile line, eventually built to 3ft 6in (both standard gauge and 4ft 0in had been proposed at times), from Wolverton to Stony

The tram operated by the Canvey Island monorail was fairly basic as illustrated here. The driver sat on the platform at the front, with the horse providing stability. *C. Carter Collection/Online Transport Archive*

The Nottingham & District Tramways Co employed steam traction for a period through until 1889. *Barry Cross Collection/Online Transport Archive*

The Bristol Tramways Co Ltd used steam traction briefly on the Horfield section during 1880 and 1881. *Barry Cross Collection/Online Transport Archive*

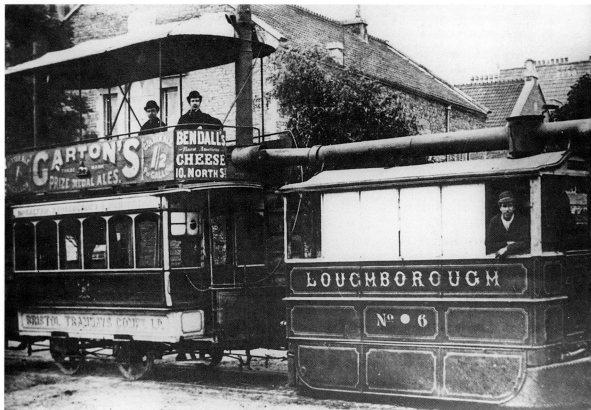

Stratford opened on 27 May 1887 under the control, now, of the Wolverton & Stony Stratford District Light Railways Co Ltd. The line was extended by two miles in 1888 to Deanshanger. However, the line failed financially and was closed by the Official Receiver on 17 December 1889. The original line reopened on 20 November 1891 with a new company — the Wolverton & Stony Stratford & District New Tramway Co — taking over on 15 September 1893. This company failed on 17 July 1919 with the line being acquired by the London & North Western Railway in February 1920 and, thus, by the LMS at Grouping in 1923. Bus competition gradually made the line uneconomic, but it was the onset of the General Strike on 4 May 1926 that saw the service end; it was not reinstated after the strike ended.

The first steam trams in Birmingham were operated by the Birmingham & Aston Tramways Co. The first section of the company's 3ft 6in network — from Aston Street in central Birmingham to Witton via two routes — opened on 26 December 1882; on 23 February 1885 a branch serving Gravelly Hill opened. The company's assets passed either to Aston Manor UDC on 30 June 1902, which then leased them to the City of Birmingham Tramways Co, or to Birmingham Corporation on 1 January 1904. Steam tram operation over the company's erstwhile routes operated between Aston Cross and Graveley Hill ceased on 13 November 1904.

Promoted by the Great Eastern Railway, the Wisbech & Upwell commenced operation between Wisbech and Outwell on 20 August 1883; it was

This view taken outside the Foresters Arms in Stony Stratford sees one of the five passenger cars supplied by the Shrewsbury-based Midland Carriage & Wagon Co for the opening of the Wolverton & Stony Stratford Tramway; it could accommodate 100 passengers and was 44ft in length. The locomotive was supplied by Thomas Green & Son in 1887. *Barry Cross Collection/Online Transport Archive*

The Birmingham & Aston Tramways Co employed a total of 27 steam tram locomotives; No 21, illustrated here, was one of 11 manufactured by Kitson & Co in 1886. *Barry Cross Collection/Online Transport Archive*

extended to Upwell on 8 September 1884. Passenger services were to survive until 31 December 1927, but freight was to continue through until 23 May 1966. The line was operated by steam tram engines with three being completed prior to the line's opening specifically for the line — GER Nos 131-33. Over the years, a number of differing tram engine types were operated before dieselisation in the early 1950s.

Following the Staffordshire Tramways Order of 1879, the first section of the 3ft 6in gauge South Staffordshire & Birmingham District Steam Tramways Co — from New Inns, Handsworth, to Darlaston via West Bromwich and Wednesbury — commenced operation on 16 July 1883. Over the next 30 months, a number of extensions were opened, taking the company's network to some 23 route miles. The company became the South Staffordshire Tramways

Co on 26 August 1889 and the process of converting the network to electric operation commenced soon afterwards. The last steam trams operated on 21 July 1907; by this date a number of sections — including those in Walsall (where steam operation ceased in 1901) — had been taken over by the local councils.

One of the shortest-lived tramways to feature in this volume was the Alford & Sutton Tramway. This was a 2ft 6in gauge line that linked Sutton-on-Sea with the main-line railway at Alford. The eight-mile line had been authorised by an Act of 12 August 1880 and opened on 2 April 1884. However, its usefulness declined in 1886 following the opening of the standard gauge Sutton & Willoughby Railway and the Alford & Sutton Tramway sought powers to abandon its line. Although the date of final operation was not recorded, the *Lincoln Gazette* of 7 December 1889

A passenger train, hauled by one of the original trio of locomotives built at Stratford in 1883, awaits departure from Upwell on the Wisbech & Upwell. *Barry Cross Collection/Online Transport Archive*

Pictured towards the end of steam operation, after the operator had been acquired by BET, South Staffs No 28, built by Beyer, Peacock, along with a Starbuck-built trailer, are pictured at the Tipton Road, Dudley, terminus of the service to Dudley and Wednesbury. *Barry Cross Collection/ Online Transport Archive*

The Alford & Sutton Tramway employed three locomotives during its relatively short life; No 2 was one of two supplied by Merryweather & Sons for the line's opening in 1884. The passenger stock consisted of four four-wheel and one bogie carriages. *Barry Cross Collection/ Online Transport Archive*

noted that operation had ceased 'ostensibly for the winter months, but really for an indefinite period'. In reality, operation was never resumed.

Although Coventry never possessed a horse tramway, it did see the operation of steam trams courtesy of the Coventry & District Tramways Co. These commenced operation over a 3ft 6in gauge line between Coventry and Bedworth, a distance of 5¾ miles, on 20 September 1884. In all, some seven locomotives plus six trailers were operated, but the line was never a great success and operation ceased completely in 1893.

The Dudley & Stourbridge Steam Tramways Co was authorised by an Order of 1881 to build 3ft 6in tramways linking Dudley, Stourbridge and Kingswinford. The Dudley to Stourbridge section opened on 21 May 1884, but the link to Kingswinford was never built. This resulted in a line of just over 5½ route miles. The company was acquired by

BET on 2 April 1898 with a view to electrification and the last steam trams operated on 25 July 1899.

Steam tram operation made a brief appearance in Plymouth beginning on 4 November 1884, when services were introduced by the Plymouth, Devonport & District Tramways on a 3ft 6in gauge line, extending for almost 2½ miles, from Mannamead via North Road to North Bay. The service was not a success and was withdrawn just over a year later, on 14 November 1885.

The Birmingham & Suburban Tramways Co was established in 1881; renamed the Birmingham Central Tramways Co Ltd two years later, the company constructed a number of 3ft 6in lines, including those along Coventry Road, Stratford Road and Moseley Road as well as routes to Perry Barr and Witton. Although horse operation had commenced earlier in the year, steam power was introduced on 25 November 1884.

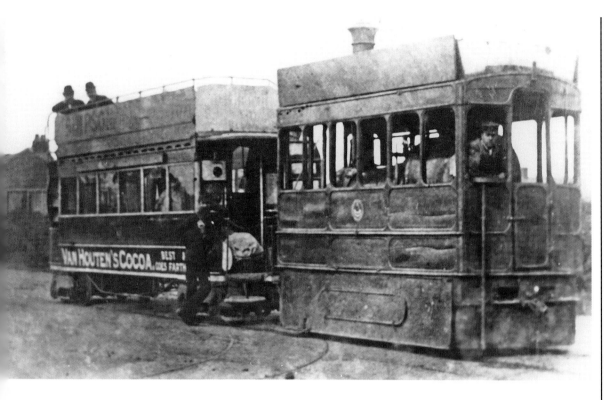

The company acquired the standard gauge lines of the Birmingham Tramways & Omnibus Co in 1886, converting them to 3ft 6in. Ownership of the company passed to the City of Birmingham Tramways Co Ltd on 15 October 1896. The new owners operated steam trams through to 31 December 1906.

A third steam tram operator in Birmingham was the Birmingham & Midland Tramways Ltd. In 1881 the Birmingham & Western Districts

The Birmingham Central Tramways Co Ltd introduced steam trams to Birmingham in 1884; locomotive No 45 was one of 29 Falcon-built locomotives delivered during 1885 and 1886. In all the company employed some 70 locomotives. Trailer No 63 was one of 64 supplied by Falcon between 1884 and 1886. *Barry Cross Collection/Online Transport Archive*

In 1896 the City of Birmingham Tramways Co Ltd took over Birmingham Central; No 40 was another of the Falcon-built steam engines and is pictured with a service towards Moseley. The last steam trams operated in Birmingham December 1906. *Barry Cross Collection/Online Transport Archive*

Tramways Co Ltd obtained powers to construct a 28-route-mile network linking Kings Heath to Dudley via Birmingham centre and associated branches. The Birmingham & Midland commenced operation on 6 July 1885, on a section of 3ft 6in line from Summer Row to the borough boundary on the Dudley Road. The company's main route was eventually extended through to Dudley with two branches serving West Bromwich (from Smethwick and from Oldbury). In all the company operated over some 12½ route miles, but the two branches to West Bromwich were not commercially successful and closed in 1892. They were reopened in May 1893 with services leased to B. Crowther; he operated the two routes with horse trams through to 1903 when they were electrified. Company steam tram operation ceased in late 1904 with the electrification of the line between Birmingham and Dudley.

The 3ft 0in Rye & Camber Tramway extended for 1¾ miles between Rye station and Camber Sands with one intermediate station at Golf Links. Designed by Holman F. Stephens and built entirely on private land — thus requiring no powers for construction — between January and July 1895, the line was designed to provide a service for golfers and holidaymakers. The section from Rye to the golf club opened in 1895; that from the club to Camber Sands followed in 1908. Passenger services were steam-hauled from the outset but were supplemented from 1924 by a petrol-driven engine. Passenger services were suspended on 4 September 1939 — never to resume — although the line was to see considerable use for military purposes during the Second World War, particularly in connection with the PLUTO (Pipe Line Under The Ocean) project. In a poor condition after the war, reopening was impractical and the line was dismantled for scrap in 1947.

The Birmingham & Midland Tramways employed 36 locomotives whilst it operated steam trams alongside 32 trailers built between 1885 and 1900. Trailer No 5 was one of 16 supplied by the Oldbury Railway Carriage & Wagon Co Ltd for the line's opening in 1885. *Barry Cross Collection/Online Transport Archive*

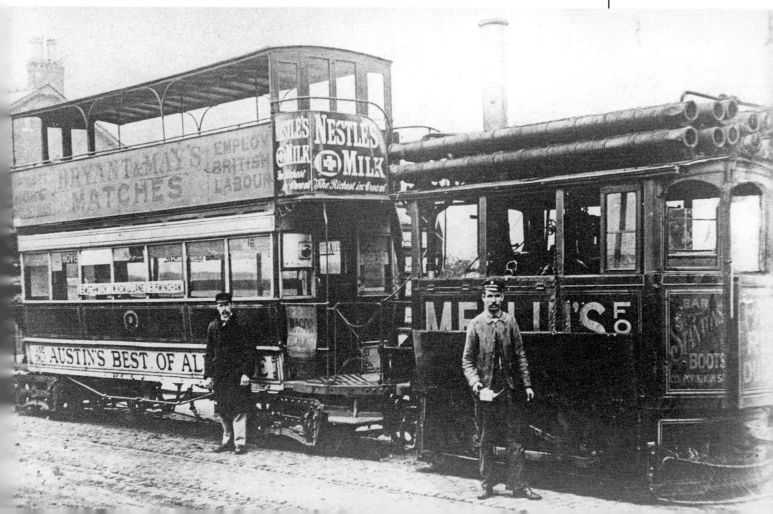

In 1892 steam tram operation on the two Birmingham & Midland Tramways' branches to West Bromwich ceased, with horse trams being employed from May 1893. Pictured in West Bromwich in 1903 — shortly before they ceased operation — is one of the horse trams operated over the routes. In the background is an electric tram from the South Staffordshire company. *Barry Cross Collection/Online Transport Archive*

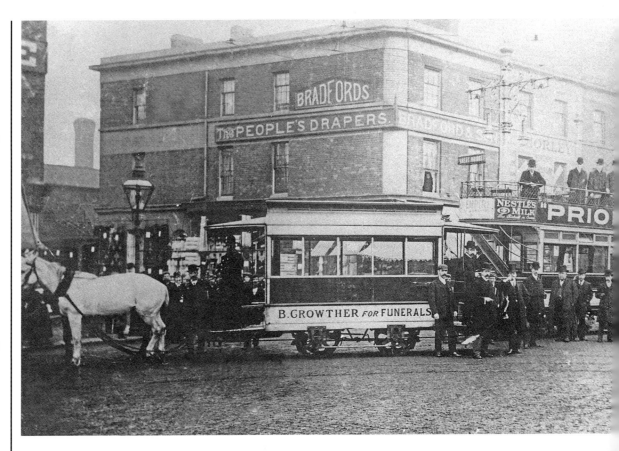

The Rye & Camber possessed two Bagnall-built 2-4-0Ts — *Camber* from 1895 and *Victoria* from 1897 — and two enclosed carriages — one built by Bagnall and the other by the Rother Iron Works. Here *Camber* stands at the basic Camber Sands station with the two carriages. *Barry Cross Collection/Online Transport Archive*

The Birmingham Tramways & Omnibus Co was acquired by the Birmingham Central Tramways Co Ltd in January 1886; the new owners undertook the conversion of the standard gauge lines to 3ft 6in and, on 24 March 1888, introduced cable traction to the Hockley route. Ownership of Birmingham Central passed to the City of Birmingham Tramways Co Ltd on 15 October 1896 and cable trams were to operate over this route until replaced by electric trams on 30 June 1911.

The longest-surviving cable tramway in England was that which served Matlock in Derbyshire. Promoted by local businessman Sir George Newnes, the ¾-mile long standard gauge route linked Crown Square with Rutland Street and was, in its time, the steepest tramway

operating on the public highway with a maximum gradient of 1 in 5½. Opened under the aegis of the Matlock Cable Tramway Co Ltd on 28 March 1893, ownership passed as a gift by Newnes to Matlock UDC in 1898, after he had bought out the other shareholders, and the service survived until 30 September 1927 when it was replaced by buses operated by North Western Road Car Co.

Prior to the introduction of overhead electric tramcars, a number of systems experimented with a number of alternative means of providing power. One of these was the Birmingham Central Tramways Co Ltd. On 24 July 1890, the company introduced battery-powered trams to the Bournbrook route. A number of self-propelled trams were acquired for

The Rye & Camber acquired a four-wheel petrol-driven Simplex-type locomotive to supplement the two steam locomotives. Built by the Kent Construction Co in 1924, the locomotive is seen at Rye with the line's engine shed beyond. *Barry Cross Collection/Online Transport Archive*

Pictured in 1896, shortly before the takeover by the City of Birmingham Tramways Co Ltd, Birmingham Central Tramways cable tram No 79 was one of 20 — Nos 75-94 — supplied by Falcon in 1888. *Barry Cross Collection/Online Transport Archive*

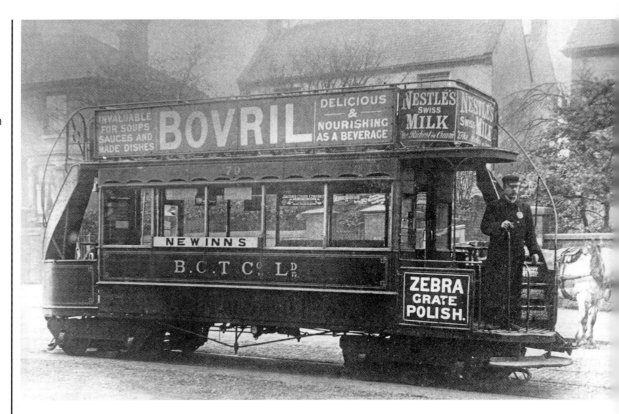

the purpose as was a battery electric locomotive (in 1892). Again inherited by the City of Birmingham Tramways

Co in 1896, the operation of battery (or accumulator) trams ceased on 12 May 1901.

The first overhead electric tramcar operation in the region covered in this

Two of the fleet of trams operated by the Matlock Cable Tramway Co Ltd — Nos 2 and 3 — pass at the Smedley Street loop. The date is *circa* 1901. Three trams were supplied by Milnes for the line's opening in 1893. *Barry Cross Collection/Online Transport Archive*

South Staffordshire
No 44 was one of 16 Brush-built trams transferred to the company between 1907 and 1912 from either the City of Birmingham or Birmingham Midland companies to replace some of the original fleet supplied in 1892. Originally open top, all of the second-hand trams were fitted with open balcony top covers as illustrated here. *Barry Cross Collection/ Online Transport Archive*

volume — indeed only the second tramway powered by this method in Britain — was that operated by the South Staffordshire Tramways Co. Its first 3ft 6in routes — Darlaston to Mellish Road and Bloxwich to Wednesbury — commenced operation on 1 January 1893. The company — which was taken over by BET in 1897 and renamed the South Staffordshire Tramways (Lessee) Co Ltd two years later — operated a network that extended over 18¼ route miles in Dudley, Walsall, Wednesbury and West Bromwich. Walsall Corporation assumed operation of part of the system in 1904 and Birmingham Corporation took over certain sections on behalf of West Bromwich Corporation during the 1920s, but it was not until 30 September 1930 that the final company trams operated with the transfer of the last sections to Walsall Corporation.

The South Staffordshire operation was one of the BET-owned companies that were to form part of the Birmingham &

Midland Tramways Joint Committee. Other participants were the Birmingham District Power & Traction Co Ltd, the Wolverhampton District Electric Tramways Ltd and the Dudley, Stourbridge & District Electric Traction Co Ltd (plus subsidiaries). A central workshop was established at Tividale, near Dudley, which operated between 1905 and September 1930 (and was used for scrapping of trams thereafter), where much of the committee's fleet was constructed. Trams carried a common livery, with allocation being indicated by the use of initials — 'SS', 'BD', 'WD' or 'DS' — on the rocker panels. The staff also wore a common uniform. The committee's operations declined as the individual company operations were either taken over by the local authorities or by conversion to bus operation.

Electric tramcar operation in Walsall commenced on 1 January 1893, courtesy of the South Staffordshire Tramways. The corporation acquired the tramways on

1 January 1901, but operation was leased to the company until 1 January 1904 when the corporation took over. During this three-year period, the corporation had built a number of new routes — again leased until 1 January 1904 — to the company. Further sections of the company's network were taken over when the corporation acquired the lines to Wednesbury, to Darlaston and the link between Darlaston and Wednesbury on 30 September 1930. Walsall had, by this date, commenced a programme of tramway conversion and the final trams on the route to Bloxwich were converted to trolleybus operation on 30 September 1933.

The Bristol Tramways & Carriage Co Ltd introduced standard gauge cars on 14 October 1895 to the Kingswood route. Eventually the system extended to some 31 route miles covering 12 routes. More than 230 tramcars were operated; these were all open-top and uncanopied. Even as late as 1920, the company was acquiring cars similar to those with which the system had been inaugurated, being unwilling to invest in fleet modernisation when the threat of a municipal takeover every seven years persisted. The corporation did take over, on 1 October 1937, but operation remained with the company and with the corporation acting only as a sleeping partner. In 1938, a five-stage plan for the elimination of the city's tramcars was agreed and the first routes converted to company-owned buses, but the final conversion, scheduled for October 1939, was deferred following the start of the Second World War. The end of the system came as a result of enemy action; on Good Friday, 11 April 1941, the city suffered a massive raid by the Luftwaffe that damaged the depot at Bedminster and demolished St Philips Bridge, thereby severing power cables that linked the power station to the Hanham and Kingswood routes. Bristol trams were never to operate again.

Walsall Corporation
No 12 was one of 28 trams supplied by Brush in 1903; originally open top, all were to receive top covers between 1904 and 1912. No 12 was one of 15 that received a Magrini open-balcony top cover between 1906 and 1910. *Barry Cross Collection/Online Transport Archive*

Typical of the Bristol fleet throughout the system's existence was No 25; this was one of some 230 virtually identical trams supplied to the company between 1895 and 1901. The last new trams — Nos 233-37 — that were built in 1920 were equally basic and were probably the last uncanopied open-top trams built for any British tramway. *S. Miles Davey/Peter Davey Collection/Online Transport Archive*

Following the demise of steam trams in Coventry, there was a brief hiatus in operation before the start of the electric tram services operated by the Coventry Electric Tramways on 5 December 1895. Initially the company operated the 5¾-mile long route north to Bedworth, but extensions followed, resulting in the company possessing just under 13 route miles when the corporation took over on 1 January 1912. The corporation inherited a fleet of 41 complete trams with one under construction. Under corporation ownership, the 3ft 6in gauge system expanded to a final route length of just over 13½ route miles, with two extensions completed in 1920 and 1929. Some of the system was converted to bus operation between 1932 and 1939, but the route to Bedworth and those to Foleshill and Bell Green were still operating on the outbreak of war, whilst the Stoke via Paynes Lane route, withdrawn in 1939, was reinstated the following year. However, Coventry was to suffer severe assault from the Luftwaffe in October and November 1940, with the result that tram services were suspended on 14 November 1940. They were never reinstated.

Powers were obtained by Dover Corporation in 1896 to construct a tramway and the first section of the 3ft 6in gauge system opened officially on 6 September 1897. Following an extension completed to the Buckland route on

The first electric trams in Coventry were operated by the Coventry Electric Tramways Ltd; this commenced services with four new trams — including No 1 — that were supplied by Brush in 1895 along with six ex-steam tram trailers, four of which were motorised. *Arthur Brookes Collection/ Online Transport Archive*

2 October 1905, the system with its main route from Minnis Lane to Clarence Place and branch to Maxton was effectively complete apart from a siding at New

Bridge opened in 1912. A total of 27 new trams were operated, the last three of which were delivered in 1920; between 1927 and 1933 older trams were replaced

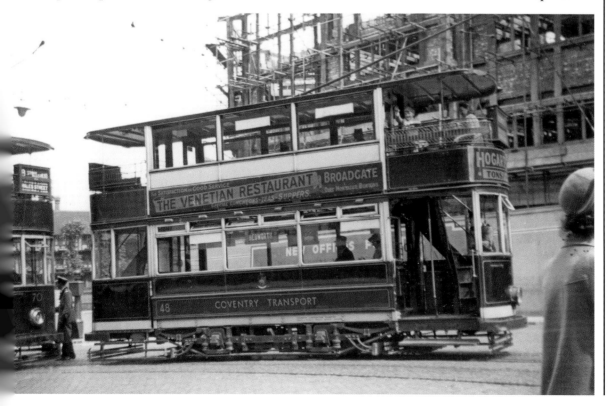

Coventry Corporation No 48 was one of seven open-balcony cars — Nos 46-52 — that were supplied by Brush on Peckham P22 trucks during 1913 and 1914. *Barry Cross Collection/ Online Transport Archive*

Two Dover trams — Nos 6 (one of 10 supplied by Brush on Peckham Cantilever trucks in 1897) and 11 (one of four built by Milnes again on Peckham Cantilever trucks the following year) — are pictured in the system's depot at Maxton. *Barry Cross Collection/Online Transport Archive*

Owned by BET, the Kidderminster & Stourport Electric Tramway Co's line was authorised in 1896 and opened from Somerleyton Avenue to Kidderminster town centre and from the town centre to Stourport on 25 May 1898. In all, the company operated just over 4½ route miles, much of it, between Stourport and Kidderminster, built alongside the road. Initially the 3ft 6in gauge line was operated by single-deck cars, including trailers, but from the early twentieth century double-deck cars also ran. A number of second-hand cars, acquired from other BET companies, supplemented the fleet. The Somerleyton Avenue section was converted to bus operation on 31 December 1923 whilst the main route to Stourport last operated on 2 April 1929.

Southampton Corporation, having acquired the Southampton Tramways Co on 1 July 1898, set about electrifying the system. The first service, from Junction to Shirley, was opened on 20 January 1900. The system continued to expand through until 10 June 1930 when the route from Bassett crossroads to Swaythling was opened; by this date the network had expanded to its maximum extent, some 13¾ route miles. Prior to the war, two services were withdrawn: Millbrook (except workmen's cars) on 2 October 1935 and Clock Tower to Northam Bridge on 4 June 1936. The onset of war saw the service to Millbrook reinstated and, to prevent potential losses, two storage sidings for the fleet were constructed in Burgess Woods. The ultimate fate of the system was, however, also to be determined during the war; in 1944 the chairman of the Transport Committee announced that the trams were to be withdrawn as part of the city's post-war reconstruction. At that stage, whether the replacements were to be bus or trolleybus — for which powers had been obtained in 1937 — was uncertain.

To serve Stoke-on-Trent, BET established the Potteries Electric Traction Co in June 1898. It took over the operation of the North Staffordshire Tramways Co as well

and the fleet was supplemented by the acquisition of no fewer than 18 second-hand trams. However, in 1934, the future of the tramway was under some doubt and it was agreed that the trams be replaced by buses operated by the East Kent Road Car Co Ltd. The final trams operated on 31 December 1936. Dover was the scene of one of Britain's worst tramway disasters when, on 19 August 1917, 11 were killed and 60 injured when No 20 ran away down Crabble Hill and overturned.

Pictured in the High Street in Stourport is Kidderminster & Stourport No 24; this tram was constructed by ERTCW and acquired by the operator in 1901. *Barry Cross Collection/Online Transport Archive*

The Bargate   Southampton

Passing through the Bargate — a mediaeval gate now listed as Grade 1 — is Southampton No 18. Following demolition of surrounding buildings, southbound trams were diverted to the east of the gate in 1932 and northbound to the west six years later. No 18 was one of the first 20 electric trams supplied to the corporation by Milnes in 1900. *Barry Cross Collection/ Online Transport Archive*

The last wholly new tram acquired by the Potteries Electric Traction Co Ltd was No 125; it was constructed at the Birmingham & Midland Tramway Co's works at Tividale in 1920 and is seen here when new. During its 29-year career, the Potteries Electric Traction Co Ltd operated an exclusively single-deck fleet. *Barry Cross Collection/ Online Transport Archive*

as the powers obtained in 1896 by Longton Corporation to construct an electric tramway. The first section of the company's 4ft 0in gauge tramway operated from Stoke to Longton on 16 May 1899. The last extension opened in 1904, taking the system to 32 route miles. In all, some 120 passenger trams were operated by the company before the final services operated on the Hanley to Newcastle service on 11 July 1928. The trams were replaced by company-owned buses; in 1933, the company was renamed the Potteries Motor Traction Co.

The steam-operated Dudley & Stourbridge Steam Tramways Co Ltd was acquired by BET in 1899 and was renamed the Dudley, Stourbridge & District Electric Traction Co Ltd. Electric services were introduced on the 3ft 6in network on 28 July 1899. Eventually the company operated over almost 23 route miles, over track owned by the company, Dudley Corporation and the Birmingham District Power & Traction Co Ltd. Conversion to

bus operation commenced in the 1920s and the last trams operated on 1 March 1930.

In 1896, Plymouth Corporation obtained powers to electrify its existing 3ft 6in gauge horse tramways. The first section of electric tram — from Theatre Royal to Prince Rock — commenced operation on 22 September 1899. The corporation was one of three operators of electric trams in the city; it was not until 1914 that Plymouth united with the neighbouring boroughs of Devonport and Stonehouse. The Plymouth, Devonport & Stonehouse Tramways Co replaced and extended its single standard gauge horse tram route with a 3ft 6in gauge electric tramway; this commenced operation on 18 November 1901. The route — just over 1¾ miles in length — was taken over by the corporation on 1 July 1922. In Devonport, the 3ft 6in gauge Devonport & District Tramways Co, a BET subsidiary, commenced electric tram operation on 26 June 1901. In all, the company

Dudley, Stourbridge & District No 2 was one of four trams that formed the 'Lye' class and were built by the Birmingham & Midland Tramways Ltd at its Tividale works. Nos 1 and 2 were transferred to Birmingham & Midland in 1925. *W. S. Eades/Online Transport Archive*

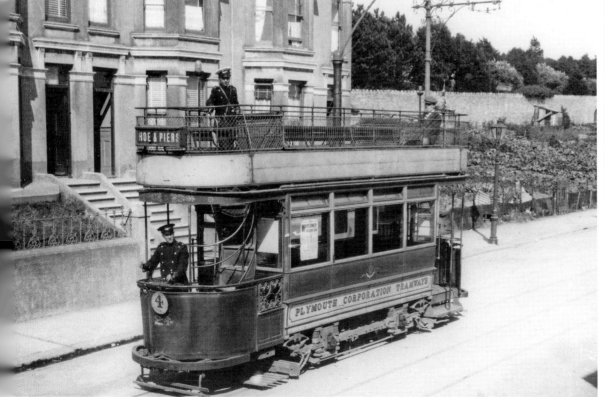

Plymouth Corporation No 24 is pictured at the Jephson Road terminus in 1921 prior to the opening of the extension to Heathfield Road. No 24 was one of 10 trams, probably built by Brush, delivered in 1902. *Barry Cross Collection/Online Transport Collection*

Plymouth, Stonehouse & Devonport No 4 was one of 12 trams supplied by ERTCW for the opening of the route in 1901. All but one of the company's fleet of 16 trams passed to the corporation in 1922. *Barry Cross Collection/Online Transport Archive*

In all the Devonport & District Tramways Co possessed 33 trams; No 4, seen here at the Stuart Road terminus, was one of 20 supplied by the J. G. Brill Co of Philadelphia in 1900. The bulk of the fleet was incorporated eventually into the corporation fleet following the latter's takeover in 1915. *Barry Cross Collection/Online Transport Archive*

operated over almost 9¼ route miles before operation passed to Plymouth Corporation in October 1915. With the takeover of the erstwhile Devonport company lines, two connections were opened at Peverell and between Penny-come-quick and Milehouse to link the two systems. At its peak in 1930 the system extended over 17½ route miles and was operated by 135 trams. Although new trams were acquired as late as 1928, the first abandonment occurred in October 1930 with the conversion of the route from Morice Square to Saltash Passage. The fleet was further supplemented in 1932 and 1934 by the purchase of second-hand cars from Exeter and Torquay respectively but conversion of the system continued; by the outbreak of war only the service from Peverell to the Theatre remained along with a link to Milehouse depot. War resulted in the system's survival but was not without its consequences. On 29 March 1941, No 153 was destroyed in a German raid whilst No 158 was damaged. The attack also led to the temporary suspension of tram services and,

when restored, a partial foreshortening of the section in the city centre.

Although Norwich had no horse trams, a significant network of electric tram routes was operated by the Norwich Electric Tramways Co. Work started on the 3ft 6in system in June 1898 and the first routes — to Dereham Road, Earlham Road, Magdalen Road and Thorpe Road — commenced operation on 30 July 1900 with further routes following on. In all, the system extended to almost 15¼ route miles. Initially, 40 motor and 10 trailer cars were supplied; these were supplemented by two motor trams acquired second-hand from Coventry. Five motor cars were modified in 1906 and transferred to Coventry; in their place five of the trailer cars were motorised with the other five being scrapped. During the 1920s, the bulk of the fleet was replaced, with the last new tram being delivered in 1930. The company was acquired by the Eastern Counties Omnibus Co in 1933 and the system was gradually converted to bus operation; the last trams were operated, on the Newmarket Road route, on 10 December

Norwich Electric Tramways Co No 35 was one of 40 trams supplied by Brush on Peckham Cantilever trucks for the system's opening; there were also 10 trailers although the use of these was limited and short-lived. The majority of the batch — but not No 35 — were to receive replacement English Electric bodies between 1924 and 1930. *Barry Cross Collection/Online Transport Archive*

Nottingham Corporation No 31 was one of 57 open-top trams supplied during 1900 and 1901 by ERTCW. All were fitted with Brill 21E trucks, but Nos 26-57 were more powerful, being fitted with two 35hp motors rather than two 25hp in the remainder. *Barry Cross Collection/ Online Transport Archive*

1935. The East Anglian Transport Museum owns the unrestored lower-deck body of one of the replacement cars, No 39 of 1924.

Following the takeover of the company-operated horse-trams, Nottingham Corporation took over some 19 route miles and immediately began plans to convert the system to electric traction. The first new services operated on 1 January 1901 and the system gradually expanded until it was just under 26 route miles in all. Although extensions were built into the 1920s, the last of these — ¼-mile to Wollaton Park Gates on 16 April 1927 — occurred after the first route to be converted to trolleybus operation — along the Nottingham Road on 1 April 1927. In all, some 200 passenger

cars were operated by the corporation, the last of which were acquired in 1926/1927. During the early 1930s, the system contracted, with the trolleybus becoming more significant, and the last trams operated on 5 September 1936. Of the last batch of trams to be acquired, Nos 181-200, eighteen were sold for further service in Aberdeen whilst a nineteenth was acquired as a source of spare parts. Although no Nottingham tram was preserved at closure, parts for four have subsequently been salvaged with a view to restoration.

The corporation was not the only operator of electric trams in the city. Between 4 July 1913 and, effectively, 5 October 1932 — when they were

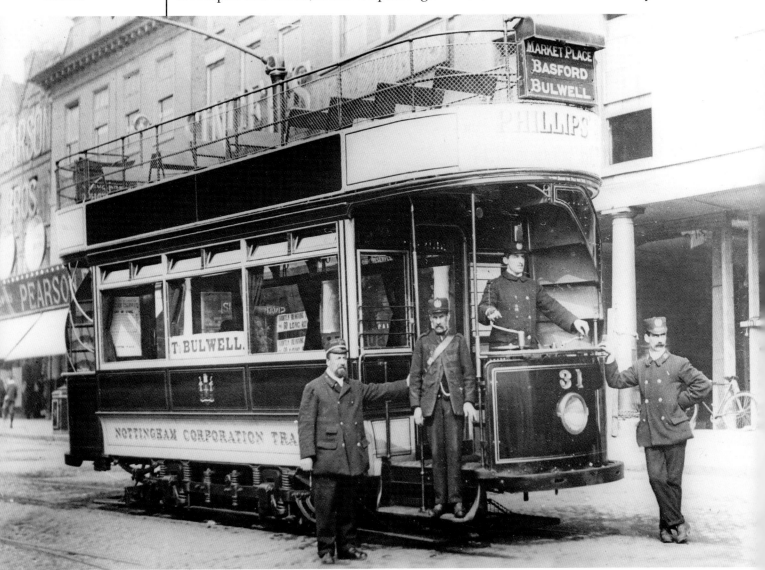

replaced by trolleybuses — trams operated by the Nottinghamshire & Derbyshire Tramway Co operated into central Nottingham over corporation-owned track. The single route — to Ripley — was but part of a grander scheme; in all the company constructed only 11 miles of the 70 route miles authorised. Following the line's completion, through services from Ripley to Nottingham commenced on 1 January 1914. In all, 24 trams were operated but, in 1928, the company obtained powers to operate trolleybuses. These were first introduced in 1931 and, on 30 December 1932, tramway operation effectively ended. For legal reasons, one tram per day ran until 5 October 1933.

Following powers granted in 1897, the Isle of Thanet Electric Tramways & Lighting Co — the Isle of Thanet Electricity Supply Co from 1924 — commenced operation of its 3ft 6in gauge line linking Ramsgate with Margate on 4 April 1901. In total the route extended just under 11 miles and a fleet of 60 trams was acquired between 1901 and 1903 to operate it. Although the tramway survived the First World War and underwent some modernisation in the 1920s, by the mid-1930s its condition was deteriorating and the local authorities petitioned the company in 1935 to replace the trams with buses. The last trams operated on 27 March 1937; the company's fleet of buses was sold to the East Kent

In all Notts & Derby employed 24 trams, all of which were supplied by UEC. Nos 1-12 were open top whilst Nos 13-24 were fitted with open-balcony top covers. All were fitted with Peckham P22 trucks. *Barry Cross Collection/Online Transport Archive*

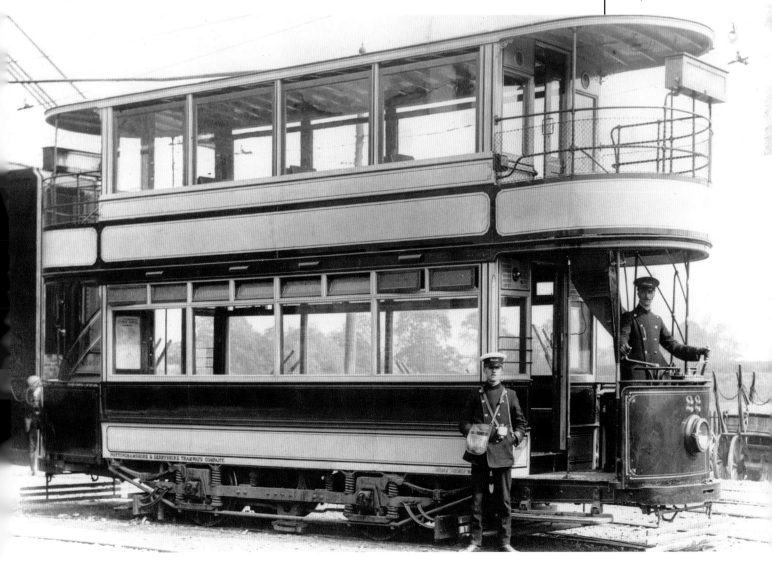

Numerically, No 60 was the highest numbered passenger car in the Isle of Thanet fleet; it was one of 10 — Nos 51-60 — open-top trams supplied by BEC in 1903. No 60 is seen here after conversion into a works car. *Barry Cross Collection/Online Transport Archive*

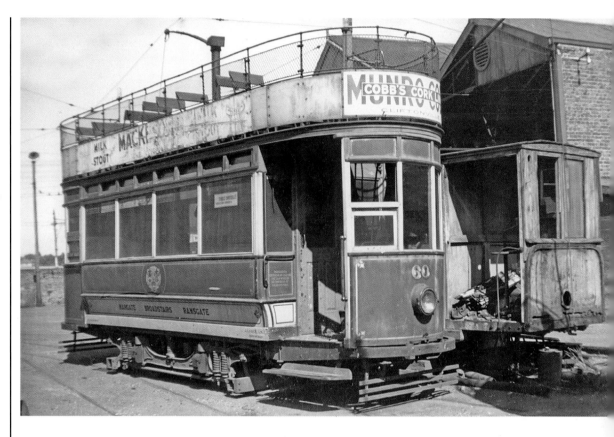

Road Car Co, which operated the route thereafter.

The Kinver Light Railway, a 3ft 6in gauge line that commenced operation on 4 April 1901, extended for almost 4¼ miles between Amblecote, where it connected with the Dudley, Stourbridge & District Electric Traction Co, and Kinver. A subsidiary of BET, ownership passed to the Dudley company — another BET subsidiary — in 1902. Passenger traffic ceased on 8 February 1930 but freight — which had also been carried — was to linger on until 1 March 1930.

The first electric trams to operate in Birmingham commenced, courtesy of the City of Birmingham Tramway Co, on the route to Bournbrook on 14 May 1901. The first corporation-operated electric trams operated on 4 January 1904 and the network expanded both through extensions but also through the take-over of erstwhile company lines as the leases on the latter gradually expired. In addition, the boundaries of the city expanded with the result that company

operations in districts such as Erdington and Yardley also passed to the corporation. The final City of Birmingham Tramway Co operations — the last company routes in the city — passed to the corporation on 31 December 1911. The system continued to expand both before and after the First World War with the last extension — the branch to Fort Dunlop — being opened on 13 February 1930, although one route — that to Nechells — was converted to trolleybus operation in 1922 (the first tram to trolleybus conversion in Britain). Two routes — Bolton Road and Bearwood — were converted to bus operation in 1930, whilst trolleybuses took over the Coventry Road route in 1934. The rest of the decade witnessed further conversions, partly the result of the desire of areas outside the city's boundaries (such as Dudley, Smethwick and West Bromwich) to see trams eliminated from their streets. As a result of these conversions, much of the network to the north and west of the city had disappeared, but the planned conversion of the Lodge Road and

The Kinver Light Railway opened with three single-deck trams — Nos 1-3 — that were supplied by Brush on Brush-built bogies. These were to become Nos 49-51 when acquired by the Dudley, Stourbridge & District Electric Traction Co Ltd in 1902. *W. S. Eades Collection/Online Transport Archive*

Birmingham Corporation No 227 is seen in Erdington High Street; this tram was one of 80 open-top cars — Nos 221-300 — supplied by UEC during 1907 and 1908. All were fitted with open-balcony top covers between 1911 and 1925. *Barry Cross Collection/Online Transport Archive*

Southend Corporation No 50 was one of 12 trams — Nos 44-55 — that were supplied by Brush and fitted with Peckham P23 maximum traction bogies. Whilst the upper decks were fully enclosed, the driving platforms were left open. From the late 1920s onwards platform vestibules were added to most — but not all — of the batch. No 50 was one of those not modified and was scrapped in 1939. *Barry Cross Collection/Online Transport Archive*

Ladywood services was deferred as a result of the war. Birmingham was an inevitable target during the war and the trams were to suffer as a consequence; in all, 22 trams were destroyed by enemy action. One section of route — from Aston to Witton — was also to close (in 1941).

Another of the few tramway systems to close during the Second World War was Southend-on-Sea. Here the corporation introduced 3ft 6in gauge electric trams on 19 July 1901, with the system continuing to expand through to the outbreak of the First World War, resulting in a network of 9¼ route miles. After the war, new trams were acquired through to 1923 and older vehicles underwent modification between 1925 and 1927. In 1925 the corporation decided to experiment with trolleybus operation and, on 28 December 1928, the first tram to trolleybus conversion took

place. Although seven second-hand trams were acquired in 1934, the policy was now to see all trams replaced. Part of the system was converted to bus operation on 6 July 1938 and a further section to trolleybus operation on 3 June 1939. Without the outbreak of war, Southend's surviving trams would have succumbed more quickly; as it was, the Ministry of War Transport gave consent for the final abandonment, and the last trams operated on 8 April 1942.

At just over 1½ route miles, the single service operated by the Taunton Electric Traction Co, a subsidiary of BET, can claim to be the shortest urban electric tramway operated in the British Isles. The route opened on 21 August 1901 and was served initially by six open-top double-deck cars. These were sold for further service to Leamington & Warwick in 1905 and

Wishing you a Happy New Yea...

Taunton. Fore Street and Burmah Cross.

replaced by six single-deck cars. When the last trams operated on 28 May 1921, five of the six cars were sold for further service (two to Gravesend and three to Torquay).

Promoted by the Cheltenham & District Light Railway, the first electric trams operated in Cheltenham on 22 August 1901. Eventually, almost 10½ route miles were operated by a fleet of twenty-five 3ft 6in gauge trams, the last two of which were acquired second-hand from Worcester in 1928. The company was owned by Balfour Beatty from 1914. In 1929, plans were unveiled to introduce trolleybuses, but these failed to progress and the trams were eventually replaced by buses. The last trams operated on 31 December 1930. Some years after withdrawal, the body of No 21 was rescued and fully restored.

Following powers obtained in 1898, Portsmouth Corporation took over the company-operated horse tramway within its boundaries on 1 January 1901. Work commenced on converting the system to electric traction and the official opening occurred on 24 September 1901 when No 1 ran from North End depot to Clarence Pier. The 4ft 7¾in gauge system continued to expand until 1913, when it reached its maximum extent of 17¾ route miles. Initially, services were operated by 80 new double-deck trams supplemented by four converted horse cars. A further 16 double-deck trams followed in 1906/07. After the First World War, a single-deck tram was acquired from Southampton and 12 new trams from English Electric in 1920. In 1930 a final new car was acquired;

On a postcard franked 31 December 1905, Taunton No 2 is pictured passing the Burmah Cross on Fore Street. Brush supplied six open-top trams to the operator during 1901 and 1902; all were to be sold to the Leamington & Warwick Electrical Co Ltd in 1905, being replaced by six single-deck trams again supplied by Brush. *Barry Cross Collection/Online Transport Archive*

Cheltenham & District No 18 was one of eight open-top trams supplied by BEC in 1904. Originally fitted with Peckham Cantilever trucks, four of the batch — Nos 14-16/19 — later received replacement Brill 21E trucks. *Barry Cross Collection/ Online Transport Archive*

this was, however, not to herald a tramway renaissance as the first route conversion — Fawcett Road — to bus occurred on

19 April 1931. In 1934, following the general manager's recommendation, it was agreed to replace the remaining trams with

Portsmouth No 83 was one of four trams built originally by Milnes for the North Metropolitan Tramways Co Ltd as horse cars in 1880 and acquired in 1896, being rebuilt as electric trams in 1903. One of the quartet — No 84 — was preserved when the system closed. *Barry Cross Collection/Online Transport Archive*

trolleybuses. The first of these changeovers occurred on 4 August 1934. The last tram route — Guildhall to Eastney — was converted on 10 November 1936. After closure, one of the ex-horse cars — No 84 — was preserved whilst the 1930-built car was sold for further service to Sunderland.

Following its reconstruction, the Great Grimsby Street Tramways Co introduced electric trams to its main route from Grimsby town centre to the seafront at Cleethorpes and to the branch along Freeman Street on 1 January 1902. In 1925 Grimsby Corporation took over the section of the company's network within the town and undertook the conversion of the Freeman Street section as part of the town's first trolleybus route; this commenced operation on 3 October 1926. The company continued operation of the

section in Cleethorpes until November 1936 following purchase by Cleethorpes Corporation on 15 July 1936. Tram operation over the main route from Grimsby centre to Cleethorpes ceased on 17 July 1937, being replaced by a new trolleybus service.

When Portsmouth Corporation took over its sections of the Portsmouth Tramways Co network, there was a short section outside the borough that remained owned by the Provincial Tramways Co. The company had obtained powers to extend the line from Cosham to Horndean and electrify it. The 4ft 7¾in Portsdown & Horndean Light Railway formally opened on 2 March 1903. The route extended for just under six miles and the corporation had running powers over the first mile. It was

Great Grimsby No 6 was one of 22 open-top trams supplied by ERTCW in 1900; 13 of the batch, including No 6, received open balcony top covers in 1908. A total of 22 trams, again including No 6, passed to Grimsby Corporation in 1925. *Barry Cross Collection/Online Transport Archive*

Another of the original batch of 22 trams supplied to the Great Grimsby Tramways Co, No 4, is pictured after 1925 when it had passed to Grimsby Corporation ownership. It is seen on Kingsway in Cleethorpes. *Barry Cross Collection/ Online Transport Archive*

In July 1936 Cleethorpes Corporation acquired those Great Grimsby trams that had not passed to Grimsby Corporation in 1925; these included No 57. This was one of three open-balcony trams, Nos 57-59, that were built by the company itself and fitted with 21E trucks manufactured by the Wigan-based Malleable Steel Castings Co Ltd. *Barry Cross Collection*

not until 19 April 1927 that the company commenced operation into Portsmouth itself. The route was operated by sixteen open-top double-deck trams acquired in 1903 and 1905; these were supplemented by eight second-hand trams acquired between 1925 and 1930. The tram service was withdrawn on 9 January 1935, being replaced by buses operated by Southdown.

Although there were earlier proposals for a tramway in Brighton, these failed to progress and it was not until 1900 that the corporation obtained powers to operate electric trams. The first section of the 3ft 6in gauge system, along the Lewes Road, opened on 25 November 1901. By 1904,

when the last extension was completed, the system extended over 9½ route miles with a maximum fleet of 80 trams. Over the years, 166 passenger trams were operated, with replacement bodies being constructed right through until 1937. The fate of the system was the development of a co-ordination agreement with the Brighton, Hove & District Omnibus Co Ltd that resulted in the system's conversion to trolleybus operation; the last trams operated in the early hours of 1 September 1939. Although no Brighton tram was preserved at closure, the body of 1937-built No 53 was subsequently rescued and is currently under restoration.

Portsdown &
Horndean No 21 was one of two Milnes-built trams transferred from Gosport & Fareham in 1930; the two had originally been built in 1906 and were fitted with M&G 21EM trucks. *Barry Cross Collection/ Online Transport Archive*

Brighton trams from two generations stand at the Aquarium terminus. On the left is No 69; this was one of 13 — Nos 68-80 — built in the corporation's workshops on Brill 21E trucks during 1929 to 1931 whilst No 49 was one of 10 — Nos 41-50 — supplied by UEC during 1904 and 1905. Fitted with Brill 21E trucks, a number — including No 49 — were used as trailers during World War One. *Barry Cross Collection/Online Transport Archive*

In 1899 BET acquired the assets of the failed Dudley & Wolverhampton Tramways Co from the receivers; the new owners proceeded to convert the route from Dudley to the Wolverhampton boundary at Fighting Cocks to 3ft 6in and electrify it. The section from the boundary to Wolverhampton centre was acquired by the corporation. The first part of the company's system opened, operated by the Dudley, Stourbridge & District, on 3 October 1900, with the Wolverhampton District Electric Tramways Co commencing operation on 9 January 1902. Eventually the company's network extended for 15½ route miles. The bulk of the company's operations passed to Wolverhampton Corporation between 1925 and 1928, with the last trams on ex-Wolverhampton District track operating on 28 September 1928.

Wolverhampton Corporation acquired the company-owned lines within the borough on 1 May 1900. The existing standard gauge lines were converted to 3ft 6in gauge and electrified and a number of extensions were constructed. As a result of opposition to overhead, the corporation adopted the Lorain stud method of current collection and the first services were operated on 6 February 1902. Apart from one section — that from Tettenhall Road to Whitmore Reams — that had already been abandoned, all the routes were converted to conventional overhead operation in 1921. With conversion to trolleybus operation in hand, the last tram services over the original corporation network were withdrawn on 26 August 1928. However, on 1 September 1928 the corporation took over part of the Wolverhampton District network. Apart from one section, these were again converted to

Wolverhampton District Tramways Co No 8 was one of 13 open-top trams supplied by ERTCW on Brill 22E trucks in 1900/01. Four — Nos 1-4 — were transferred to Dudley, Stourbridge & District in 1904, but the remainder received extended canopies at Tividale works in *circa* 1910 with the majority receiving replacement Brush-built trucks. *Barry Cross Collection/ Online Transport Archive*

Wolverhampton Corporation No 44, one of six open-top trams supplied by UEC during 1908 and 1909 on Brill 21E trucks, is pictured whilst fitted for stud operation. *Barry Cross Collection/Online Transport Archive*

trolleybus operation, with the last trams operating over the acquired routes on 30 November 1928.

Extending for almost three miles, the 3ft 6in gauge tramway of the Weston-super-Mare & District Electricity Supply Co commenced operation on 13 May 1902. The company owned 18 trams during its history, but four of these were sold to Swansea in 1904, when barely a year old, following storm damage. The final two trams were acquired as late as 1927, but were to see barely a decade of operation as buses replaced the trams on 17 April 1937.

In north Kent, the Chatham & District Light Railways Co introduced 3ft 6in gauge trams to the Chatham and Gillingham area on 17 June 1902. The system eventually extended to almost 15 route miles, with services into Rainham, Rochester and Strood. In all, the company operated 52 passenger cars; the last new trams were delivered in 1911 but, in 1928, a second-hand car was

acquired from Maidstone Corporation. In 1927, the company was acquired by Maidstone & District Motor Services; the new owners effected some improvements but it was to be but a temporary reprieve and the last trams operated on 30 September 1930. They were replaced by the buses of the Chatham & District Traction Co (as the company had been renamed).

Both the corporation and BET vied to introduce electric trams to Bournemouth; in the event it was the former that was to prove successful, with services being introduced to the Lansdowne to Pokesdown route on 23 July 1902. Further routes were to follow, with the system being centred on The Square; from opening until 1911, when conventional overhead was installed, this section was operated by conduit. Following a decision to replace the routes within Bournemouth by trolleybus, the last tram operated on 8 April 1936. Following closure, eleven of the 3ft 6in

The last trams acquired by the Weston-super-Mare & District Electricity Supply Co were two toastracks — Nos 17 and 18 — that were supplied by Brush on Brill Radiax bogies in 1927. *Barry Cross Collection/Online Transport Archive*

gauge trams were sold for further service on the Llandudno & Colwyn Bay line from where ex-Bournemouth No 85 was eventually to be preserved.

On 16 June 1905, Bournemouth Corporation took over the 3¾ route miles operated by Poole & District Electric Tramways, a BET subsidiary, which had commenced operation originally on 6 April 1901. The corporation absorbed the company's fleet of 17 trams and constructed a connection between the two systems at Westbourne. Granted a 30-year lease, operation of the erstwhile Poole & District route ceased on 8 June 1935, on the expiry of the lease, to be replaced by company-owned buses. A second route, constructed by Poole Corporation through Lower Parkstone, opened on 3 August 1906 but this was converted to bus operation in 1929.

The 3ft 6in gauge corporation-owned electric tramways in Great Yarmouth comprised two separate and unconnected sections on the east and west side of the River Yare; these amounted in total

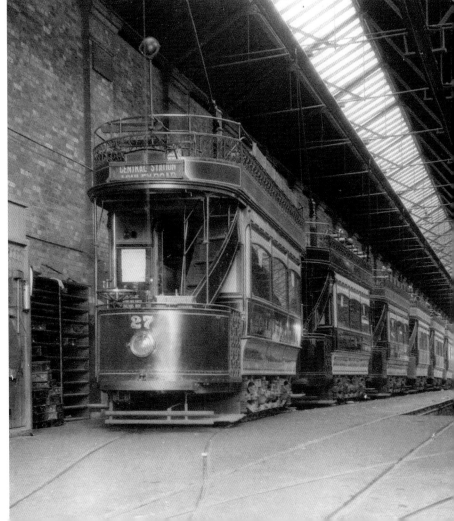

Poole & District owned 17 trams in all, including 7 — Nos 5-11 — supplied by ERTCW on Brill 21E trucks in 1901. All passed to Bournemouth Corporation in 1905, with No 11 becoming Bournemouth No 65. The ERTCW-built cars were subsequently modified with extended canopies. *Barry Cross Collection/Online Transport Archive*

to just under ten route miles. The first electric services, on 19 June 1902, ran on the eastern section. The western section was originally the horse route of the Yarmouth & Gorleston Tramway; electric trams commenced operation on this section on 4 July 1905. In all, some 35 trams were delivered between 1905 and 1907 to operate the network. The first conversion to corporation-owned buses occurred in 1924; the western section was converted on 25 September 1930 and the final trams operated on 14 December 1933.

Following the acquisition of the existing Gravesend, Rosherville & Northfleet

Tramways by the Gravesend & Northfleet Tramways Co (a BET subsidiary), the tramway was converted to standard gauge and electrified. The new electric services commenced on 2 August 1902. Following extensions opened the following year, the system reached its maximum extent of 6½ route miles. The final trams to be acquired were two second-hand from Taunton in 1921. The last trams operated on 29 February 1929.

The only electric tramway in Cornwall was the Camborne & Redruth. This 3ft 6in gauge line extended to almost 3½ route miles and was owned by the United Electric Supply Co Ltd. The line opened

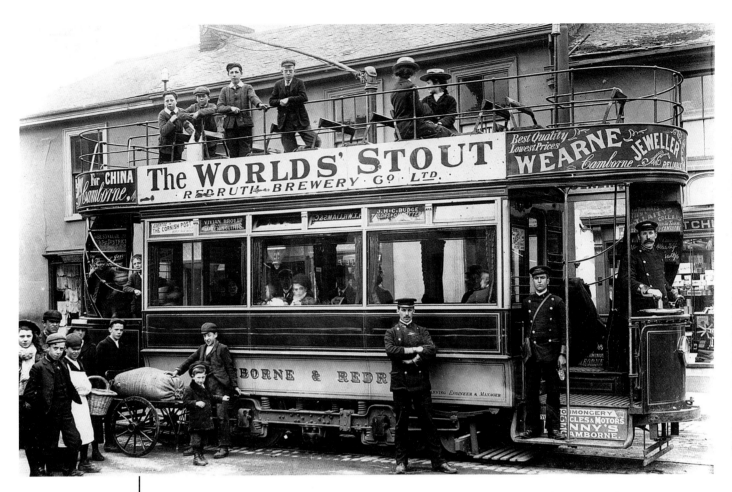

In all the Camborne & Redruth operated eight passenger trams; Nos 1-4 were built by Milnes and delivered in 1902. No 3 is recorded here in Camborne the following year. *Barry Cross Collection/ Online Transport Archive*

on 7 November 1902 and was operated by initially six trams with two more acquired the following year. Passenger services ceased on 29 September 1929 as a result of bus competition, but the freight service, carrying tin ore from two mines to the smelting works over part of the route, was to survive using electric locomotives until August 1934.

Opened on 24 January 1903, a small 3ft 6in gauge system served Peterborough courtesy of the Peterborough Electric Traction Co. The network extended over three routes — a total of just over 5¼ route miles — operated by a fleet of 14 Brush-built double-deck trams. The company introduced its first bus services in 1913, but the tramway itself was to survive until 15 November 1930.

The dubious honour of being the first electric tramway to close in the British Isles belongs to the short-lived Sheerness & District Tramways. This 2½-mile 3ft 6in

gauge line opened on 9 April 1903. Supplied with 12 trams, the line's Achilles' Heel was the fact that its overhead equipment was supplied by the German company of Siemens & Halske. This meant that it was impossible to obtain spares for the overhead following the outbreak of war in August 1914. As a result, the system was abandoned on 7 July 1917. The surviving eight cars in the fleet — Nos 9-12 had been sold in 1904 to the City of Birmingham Tramways Co Ltd — were sold to Darlington Corporation.

Electric trams were introduced to Ilkeston by the corporation on 16 May 1903. In all, thirteen 3ft 6in gauge trams operated over two lines that totalled 4¼ route miles. Never a success, operation passed to the Nottinghamshire & Derbyshire Tramway Co on 16 November 1916. The company assumed ownership of the line six years later. The last

Peterborough Electric Traction Co No 6 — one of 14 open-top double-deck trams supplied to the operator by Brush — is pictured at the terminus at Dogsthorpe. *Barry Cross Collection/ Online Transport Archive*

Sheerness & District No 4 was one of twelve Brush-built trams operated by the company; following closure, the surviving cars was sold to Darlington Corporation. *Barry Cross Collection/ Online Transport Archive*

Ilkeston Corporation No 5 is pictured on Bath Street on 16 May 1903. This was one of nine open-top trams supplied by ERTCW in 1902; these and a further four trams supplied by Milnes in 1903 passed to Notts & Derby in November 1916. *Barry Cross Collection/Online Transport Archive*

trams operated on 15 January 1931 to be replaced by company-owned trolleybuses.

More than a year after electric trams were introduced to neighbouring Great Yarmouth, the first 3ft 6in gauge trams commenced operation in Lowestoft on 22 July 1903. The corporation-operated network extended over four route miles with a fleet of fifteen double-deck and four single-deck trams. The last trams operated on 8 May 1931, being replaced by corporation-owned buses. One of the Milnes-built double-deck cars, No 14, was rescued for preservation in 1962 and is undergoing long-term restoration at Carlton Colville. The East Anglian Transport Museum also owns the restored but grounded body of one of the four single-deck cars.

Another operator to commence operation on 22 July 1903 was the only electric network in Berkshire, that of Reading Corporation. Following the takeover of the assets of the Reading Tramways Co on 1 November 1901, the corporation proceeded to electrify the existing route and construct extensions. Eventually, the 4ft 0in gauge network extended to 7½ route miles operated by 36 passenger cars: 30 four-wheel and six bogie cars. All bar one of the former were rebuilt between 1920 and 1929. The first conversions — to bus — occurred in 1930 (Bath Road) and 1932 (Erleigh Road), but it was subsequently decided to replace the remaining trams with trolleybuses. These were introduced to the Caversham Road route in place of trams on 18 July 1936 and the final trams operated on 20 May 1939.

LOWESTOFT. LONDON ROAD, N. 32.

Lowestoft Corporation No 7 is pictured on London Road North; the system's main route linked Pakefield, south of the river, with Lowestoft North station. Milnes supplied 11 open-top trams — Nos 1-11 — for the opening of the system in 1903. *Barry Cross Collection/Online Transport Archive*

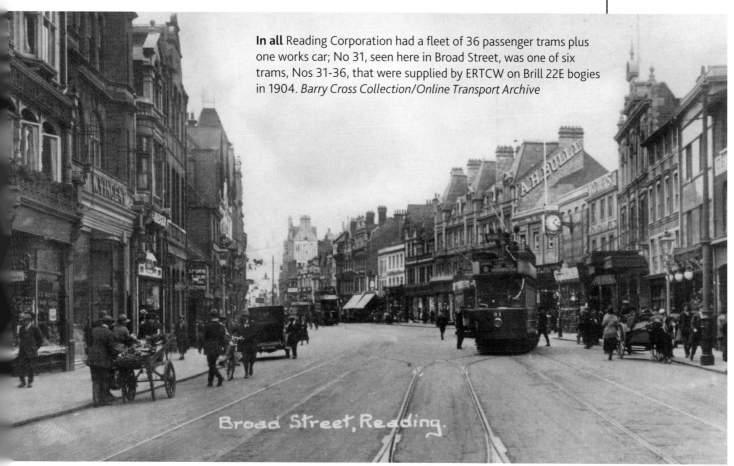

Broad Street, Reading.

In all Reading Corporation had a fleet of 36 passenger trams plus one works car; No 31, seen here in Broad Street, was one of six trams, Nos 31-36, that were supplied by ERTCW on Brill 22E bogies in 1904. *Barry Cross Collection/Online Transport Archive*

Burton Corporation received 20 open-top trams from ERTCW for the system's opening in 1903; two of these, Nos 1 and 9, are seen passing near the railway station. The photograph dates prior to 1906 as No 9 was one of six of the type to receive open-balcony top covers between 1903 and 1906. *Barry Cross Collection/Online Transport Archive*

In Burton-on-Trent, the corporation introduced 3ft 6in gauge electric tramcars on 3 August 1903. In all, four routes were operated from the station to Branston Road, Horninglow, Stapenhill and Winshill, giving a route mileage of 8½ in total. The trams were converted progressively to corporation-owned buses between 1927 and 31 December 1929, when the last of the corporation's 24 tramcars — the last four of which were new only in 1920 — operated for the last time.

The Burton Corporation-owned route to Winshill was also used by the trams of the Midland Railway-owned Burton & Ashby Light Railway. This opened on 2 July 1906 and provided a connection from near the corporation terminus at Winshill through to Ashby-de-la-Zouch, with a short branch from Swadlincote to Castle Gresley. In all, 20 tramcars were supplied by Brush to operate the system. At the Grouping of the railways in 1923, ownership passed to the LMS under whose aegis the tramway was abandoned on 19 February 1927. One of the fleet — No 14 — was eventually acquired for preservation. Fitted with an ex-Lisbon truck, the tram spent some years in Detroit before being repatriated to Britain in 2014; it is now based at Statfold Barn.

Having acquired the company-owned horse tramway on 1 November 1901, Ipswich Corporation introduced electric trams to the town on 23 November 1903.

The system eventually extended to about 11 route miles, operated by 36 Brush-built open-top tramcars. Ipswich was an early operator of trolleybuses and conversion of the 3ft 6in gauge trams commenced in 1923. The last trams operated on 26 July 1926, all being replaced by trolleybuses; Ipswich remained an all-electric fleet until its first diesel buses were acquired after the Second World War. In 1976, the body of No 33 was acquired; fitted with a second-hand truck from Lisbon, restoration of the tram at the Ipswich Transport Museum was completed in 2012.

In 1902, the horse trams of the Bath Road Car & Tramways Co were taken over by the corporation to facilitate electrification. Conversion to standard gauge followed, with the first electric trams — operated by the Bath Electric Tramways Co, a BET

subsidiary — opening on 2 January 1904. The system, which extended to 14¾ route miles, comprised six routes with the last extension opening on 5 August 1905 operated by 40 trams. The company was taken over by the Bristol Tramways & Carriage Co in December 1936. The last tram operated on 6 May 1939, all being replaced by company-owned buses.

BET established the Worcester Electric Traction Co Ltd in 1902 to take over and electrify the city's horse tram system with services commencing on 6 February 1904. Following an extension in 1906, the system reached its peak of just under six route miles. Initially, fifteen 3ft 6in gauge trams entered service; these were supplemented by a further two in 1921. The trams survived until 31 May 1928 when they were replaced by buses operated by

The rural nature of much of the Burton & Ashby system is emphasised by this view of No 5; in all, Brush supplied 20 open-top trams to the company. All were fitted with Brush AA trucks. *Barry Cross Collection/Online Transport Archive*

One of the 26 open-top cars supplied by Brush on Brill 21E trucks for the introduction of electric trams to Ipswich in 1903 is pictured heading eastwards into Tavern Street from Cornhill in a postcard franked 3 August 1909. *Barry Cross Collection/Online Transport Archive*

During 1903 and 1904 Milnes supplied Bath Electric Tramways Ltd with 34 open-top double-deck and six single-deck combination cars. One of the former, No 6, is pictured heading westwards with a service to Weston. *S. Miles Davey/Peter Davey Collection/ Online Transport Archive*

Midland Red. The 1921-built trams were sold for further service to Cheltenham.

Gloucester Corporation acquired the company-owned horse trams in 1902 and proceeded to convert the system to electric traction. The first electric trams operated on 29 April 1904 and the system eventually grew to 9¾ route miles. A short section was abandoned in 1917 to permit an extension to serve the Brockworth aircraft factory, with a further ¾-mile of track installed within the factory site. The system was operated by 30 passenger cars; conversion to corporation-owned buses commenced in 1927 with the final trams operating on 11 January 1933.

Following the take-over of the company horse trams in 1902, Leicester Corporation commenced electric tramcar operation on 18 May 1904 when an official party travelled from Stoneygate to Abbey Park Road. Much of the network was opened between then and the end of 1905 but one extension opened in 1915 to be followed by three post-war: in September 1922 (Welford Road), in June 1924 (Blackbird Road) and March 1927 (Coleman Road). This took the system's route mileage to its maximum of 22¾, operated by a fleet of 178 four-wheel tramcars. Although one section of line had been converted in the early 1930s — Melbourne Road (13 December 1933) — it was the decision made after a report in 1938 advocating replacement of the city's trams by either buses or trolleybuses that sealed its fate. Two sections — Coleman Road (on 23 October 1938) and King Richard's Road (on 2 April 1939) — were converted to bus operation before the outbreak of the Second World War. War resulted in the

One of the Brush-built open-top trams delivered for the opening of the Worcester system in 1904 heads towards St Johns. In all Brush supplied 17 trams on Brush AA trucks, but only 15 entered service; the remaining two were diverted for operation in Peterborough. *Barry Cross Collection/ Online Transport Archive*

Gloucester Corporation Light Railways No 4 — one of 30 open-top trams supplied by Brush on Brush AA trucks during 1903 and 1904 — is pictured en route to Hucclecote; this route, which featured a considerable stretch of single track with passing loops, was extended in 1917 to serve the airfield at Brockworth. *Barry Cross Collection/ Online Transport Archive*

system's reprieve. The pre-war closures saw the fleet reduced by 19 trams but 159 soldiered on through the war.

On 14 July 1904, Maidstone Corporation opened its first 3ft 6in gauge route; this extended from the town centre to Barming. Two extensions — to Loose in October

1907 and Tovil in January 1908 — followed, taking the system to its maximum extent, 5¼ route miles. In all, 18 passenger cars were operated; the last to be delivered — No 18 — was a demi car for use on the unremunerative Tovil section; the body of this car was salvaged long

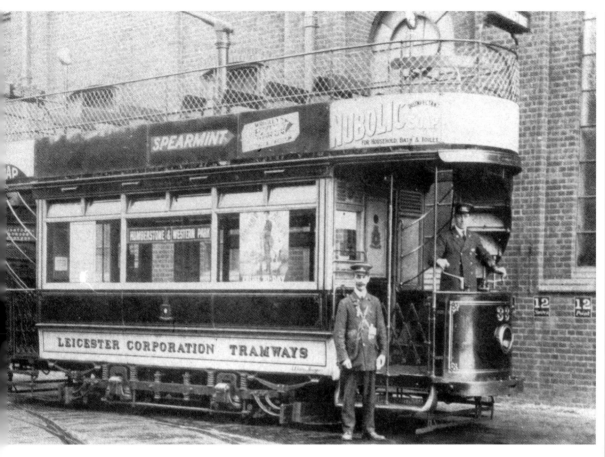

Typical of the early tramcars supplied to Leicester Corporation by ERTCW on Brill 21E trucks was No 33; in all, 99 open-top double-deck cars were supplied by the manufacturer during 1903 and 1904. All received open-balcony top covers between 1912 and 1927 and all bar six were rebuilt as fully enclosed between 1924 and 1934. *Barry Cross Collection/ Online Transport Archive*

In all, Maidstone Corporation possessed 18 passenger trams; No 12 seen here at Tovil was one of 10. Nos 8-17, supplied by UEC on Brill 21E trucks in 1907. *Barry Cross Collection/ Online Transport Archive*

During 1904 and 1905 ERTCW supplied 22 open-top trams on Brill 21E trucks to Northampton Corporation; seven — including No 5 in 1925 — were to receive open balcony top covers between 1923 and 1926. *Barry Cross Collection/Online Transport Archive*

after closure and is now based in Dover awaiting restoration. The first conversion to trolleybus occurred on 1 May 1928 with the demise of the Barming route; the Tovil route was converted to bus operation in August 1929. The last tram operated on 11 February 1930 when the Loose route was converted to trolleybus operation.

The first trams supplied to Derby Corporation were 25 open-top double-deckers supplied by ERTCW on Brush AA trucks in 1904; No 1, pictured here at the Burton Road terminus, was to receive — like the bulk of the batch — a replacement Brill 21E truck. Withdrawn in August 1933, the body of No 1 was sold for use as a summerhouse. Recovered in 1970, the vehicle was fully restored — albeit to standard gauge — and now forms part of the NTM collection. *Barry Cross Collection/ Online Transport Archive*

Northampton Corporation introduced 3ft 6in gauge electric trams to the town, following the take-over of the company-owned horse trams in 1901, on 21 July 1904. In all, some 37 tramcars were operated, the last of which were delivered in 1921 over a network that extended for some 8¼ route miles. The

Colchester Corporation No 13, seen here on St Botolphs Street, was one of 16 open-top trams supplied by ERTCW on Brill 21E trucks in 1904. *Barry Cross Collection/Online Transport Archive*

last extension, to Far Cotton, opened in 1914. The trams were replaced by corporation-owned buses, with the last operating on 15 December 1934. Although no Northampton tram was preserved on closure, the lower deck of 1905-built No 21 has been subsequently rescued but not as yet restored.

After its acquisition of the company-operated horse trams on 1 November 1899, Derby Corporation obtained powers the following year to convert the system to electric operation and to extend it. The first electric services commenced on 27 July 1904. The 4ft 0in gauge system eventually extended over some 14 route miles, with the last extension opening on 8 February 1908. In all some 78 trams were operated, with the last being acquired new in 1926 and 1927. However, two years later, on 21 August 1929, the council decided

to convert its tram system in favour of trolleybuses. Following the acquisition of powers, the first conversion took place on 9 January 1932 and the last tram operated on 2 July 1934. The body of No 1 was rescued in 1962 and subsequently restored on a standard gauge truck at Crich.

The day after the opening of the Derby system, Colchester Corporation inaugurated its own 3ft 6in gauge network. In all, three routes were constructed with a mileage of 5¾ operated by a fleet of 18 open-top ERTCW- or UEC-built tramcars. In 1927, the corporation obtained powers to replace the life-expired trams with buses and the first conversion took place on 21 May 1928. The last tram operated on the North station to Recreation Ground route on 9 December 1929. All the tram services were replaced by corporation-owned motorbuses.

Swindon No 3 heads into Park Lane with a service for Rodbourne. This tram was one of nine open-top trams supplied to the corporation by ERTCW on Brill 21E trucks during 1904 and 1905. *Barry Cross Collection/Online Transport Archive*

The only town in Wiltshire to see the operation of electric trams was Swindon, where the corporation introduced them on 22 September 1904. Eventually, almost 3¾ route miles of 3ft 6in gauge tramway were operated by a fleet of 13 open-top trams, the last of which was delivered in 1921. Unfortunately, the system suffered a major accident in 1906 when No 11 crashed, killing five. The final trams operated on 11 July 1929, being replaced by corporation-owned buses.

The company-owned horse trams in Chesterfield passed to corporation control in 1897, but it was not until 1904 that work started to convert the line to electric traction. The single route — some 3½ miles in length — from Whittington Moor to Brampton commenced operation on 20 December 1904. The corporation possessed 19 passenger trams during its life (two being added in 1920 to replace two cars destroyed by fire in 1916). The last trams operated on 23 May 1927, being replaced by corporation-owned trolleybuses. The body of No 7 was rescued in 1997 and has been fully restored at the NTM.

Following the acquisition of the company's horse trams on 1 February 1904, Exeter Corporation converted the existing routes to electric traction, including a section along the High Street that had hitherto been free from tram operation. In all, the network extended to some five route miles but, despite the purchase of new tramcars as late as 1929, increased traffic congestion and lack of maintenance resulted in the corporation deciding in 1930 to convert the system to bus operation. The last trams operated on 19 August 1931.

In 1899, BET acquired the Leamington & Warwick Tramways & Omnibus Co with a view to electrification of the three-mile 3ft 6in gauge route, Renamed the Leamington & Warwick Electrical Co in 1902, the company's electric tram service was introduced on 15 July 1905. The initial fleet of six trams was supplemented the

Chesterfield Corporation No 6 was one of 12 — Nos 1-12 — supplied by Brush on Brush Conaty trucks in 1904. Sister car No 7 — one of seven trams fitted with an open-balcony top cover during 1919 and 1920 — was rescued for preservation and restored in 1997 as part of the NTM collection. *Barry Cross Collection/Online Transport Archive*

same year by six acquired second-hand from Taunton; a thirteenth car — No 14 — was added in 1921. This had been built originally for operation at Cheltenham but diverted to Leamington before delivery.

Two of Exeter Corporation's first batch of trams — Nos 6 (to Heavitree) and 10 (to Pinhoe Road) — are seen heading eastbound along the High Street. The first 12 trams were supplied by ERTCW on Brill 21E trucks in 1905. *Barry Cross Collection/Online Transport Archive*

Leamington & Warwick No 2 was one of the six trams originally supplied to the operator by Brush in 1905. The remaining seven trams operated were acquired second-hand: six in 1905 and one in 1921. *Barry Cross Collection/ Online Transport Archive*

The service continued until 16 August 1930 when the trams were replaced by Midland Red buses.

Electric trams arrived in Mansfield, courtesy of the Mansfield & District Light Railways Co, on 16 July 1905. In all, five standard gauge routes, with a total route mileage of 12¼, radiated out from the town centre. A total of 31 tramcars were operated, three of which were acquired from Notts & Derby in 1930. Although powers to operate trolleybuses were obtained, the trams were to be replaced by company-owned buses, with the last trams operating on 9 October 1932.

The Provincial-backed Hastings, Bexhill & District Light Railways (Electric) Co Ltd — Hastings & District Electric Tramways Co Ltd from 1904 — obtained powers to construct two networks; a town system in Hastings and a separate line in Bexhill. These opened on 31 July 1905 and 9 April 1906 respectively; it would not be until 12 January 1907 that the two sections were linked. As a result of council opposition, no overhead was erected along the Promenade. From opening through to 26 March 1914, this section was operated using the unsuccessful Dolter surface stud system and then, until agreement to erect overhead was given, those Dolter-fitted cars were converted to petrol-electric, being fitted with petrol engines for the purpose; overhead was finally erected in 1921. The system extended over 19½ route miles with a total of 65 double-deck trams being owned. The company proposed modernising the tramway in the 1920s, but

Mansfield & District No 3 was one of 12 trams supplied by Hurst Nelson on Hurst Nelson-built 21E trucks in 1905. Four of the type — but not No 3 — subsequently received Peckham P22 trucks whilst a further four — again not No 3 — were to receive open balcony top covers. One of the P22-fitted trams was rebuilt as fully enclosed. *Barry Cross Collection/Online Transport Archive*

For a period the Hastings, Bexhill & District Light Railways (Electric) Co Ltd used the Dolter surface stud system along the Promenade; No 45 was one of 20 trams — Nos 41-60 — that were supplied by UEC in 1906 fitted with Dolter stud equipment from new. The majority, but not all, were operated by petrol-electric motors between 1914 and 1921. *Barry Cross Collection/Online Transport Archive*

Lincoln Corporation No 2 was one of six open-top trams supplied by Brush on Brush Conaty trucks in 1902; it is pictured during the period when the Lincoln trams operated using the Griffiths-Bedell stud system — hence the lack of a trolleypole and overhead. *Barry Cross Collection/Online Transport Archive*

agreement with the council could not be reached and so it was decided to replace the trams with trolleybuses. The last tram operated on 15 May 1929.

Having acquired the company-owned horse trams in July 1904, Lincoln Corporation undertook the electrification of the single route — from Cornhill to Bracegirdle (a distance of almost two miles) — using, unusually, the Griffiths-Bedell stud system rather than conventional overhead. Services were introduced on 23 November 1905 with a fleet of eight cars. The stud system was not wholly successful — problems with leaking gas could cause minor explosions, for example — but it was not until 1919 that it was replaced by the more usual overhead. Contemporaneously with the change, three new trams — the last to be acquired — were bought. Lincoln's trams last operated on 31 December 1929, being replaced by corporation-owned buses.

Another subsidiary of the Portsmouth Street Tramways Co introduced electric trams to Gosport in place of the earlier 3ft 0in gauge horse trams operated by the company in the town. Authorised by Acts in 1901, 1903 and 1905, the existing tramway was converted to 4ft 7¾in gauge and electrified. Services were introduced on 20 December 1905. Extensions — to Fareham and to Bury Cross — followed on 24 January 1906 and 13 October 1906 respectively. This took the system to its maximum extent — 7¾ route miles — which was operated by a fleet of 22 open-top double-deck trams. The trams last operated on 31 December 1929, to be replaced by company-owned buses. Of the fleet, seven were transferred for further

Gosport & Fareham No 8 was one of 12 Brush-built trams supplied in 1905 on Brush 21EM trucks; on the line's closure in 1929 No 8 was one of seven trams from the 22-strong fleet transferred to the Portsdown & Horndean. A further 12 were acquired by the Great Grimsby Street Tramways Co. *Barry Cross Collection/Online Transport Archive*

use on the Portsdown & Horndean line and twelve passed to the Great Grimsby Street Tramways Co.

As a result of opposition to the use of overhead, the introduction of trams to Torquay was relatively late and they required the use of the Dolter stud system of current supply rather than overhead. The first operation of the Torquay Tramways Co commenced on 4 April 1907. With the decision to extend the system into neighbouring Paignton, it was also decided to convert the Dolter stud-fitted section to conventional overhead; this work was all completed in 1911. The system extended over some nine route miles with, in all, forty-two 3ft 6in gauge trams owned. The last six trams were acquired between 1923 and 1928; following the final conversion of the system on 31 January 1934, these six cars were sold for further service to Plymouth.

Luton was a relative latecomer to the operation of trams. It was not until October 1907 that construction started, and the first services commenced on 21 February 1908. Initially, operation of the standard gauge system was leased to J.G. White & Co; the lease passed

to Balfour Beatty & Co in 1909. It was not until 21 February 1923 that Luton Corporation took over operation itself. The system extended over 5¼ route miles and was operated for the bulk of its life by 12 cars delivered for the system's opening. A thirteenth car was acquired second-hand in 1923. The last trams operated on 16 April 1932, being replaced by corporation-owned buses.

The last first-generation tramway to commence operation in the area covered by this book is the Grimsby & Immingham. The Great Central Railway undertook the development of a new dock complex at Immingham during the first decade of the twentieth century. The company recognised that it needed to provide transport for the dockworkers. Initially, from 3 January 1910, the railway provided a steam-operated service over the Grimsby District Light Railway; however, an electric tramway was constructed. This was an attractive proposition for the railway as it used electricity generated by the power station at the docks and could be extended potentially over the public highway into Grimsby itself. The first section of the line — from Corporation Bridge in

Torquay Tramways
Co Ltd No 27 was one of 15 — Nos 19-33 — that were acquired from Brush on Brill 21E trucks during 1910 and 1911. Unlike the first batch, Nos 1-18, these trams were equipped with a trolleypole from new. *Barry Cross Collection/Online Transport Archive*

Luton Corporation
No 1 was the first of 12 open-top trams supplied by UEC on M&G 21EM trucks during 1907 and 1908; it was one of four of the batch that were fitted with Brush-built top covers during 1929. *Barry Cross Collection/Online Transport Archive*

Grimsby to Immingham Town — opened on 15 May 1912; steam operation ceased the previous day. On 17 November 1913, the section from Immingham Town to Immingham Dock was opened. A short extension from Immingham Town to Queens Road was also constructed but this was never formally opened, despite being inspected on 20 July 1915. In 1923, the line, along with the rest of the Great Central Railway, passed to the London & North Eastern Railway.

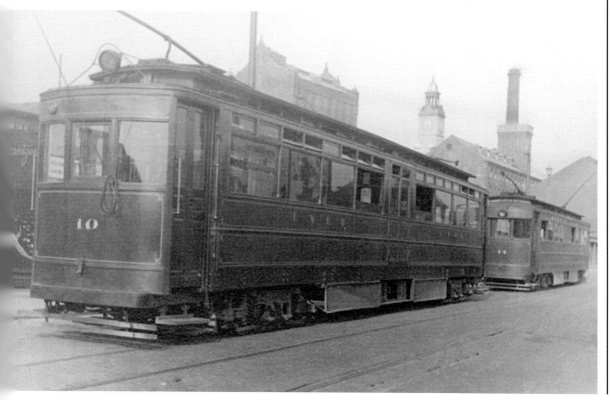

Between 1923 and 1948 the Grimsby & Immingham was operated by the LNER. Here, two of the trams acquired by the Great Central are seen at the Corporation Bridge terminus in Grimsby. No 10 was one of four Brush-built trams supplied in 1913 whilst No 14 was one of a quartet built by Brush and the GCR two years later. No 14 was to be preserved following withdrawal - the only one of the ex-GCR trams to survive. *Barry Cross Collection/Online Transport Archive*

BIRMINGHAM

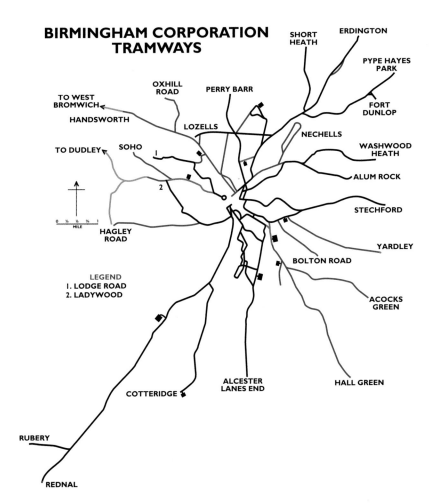

BIRMINGHAM CORPORATION TRAMWAYS

SHORT HEATH

ERDINGTON

PYPE HAYES PARK

OXHILL ROAD

PERRY BARR

TO WEST BROMWICH

HANDSWORTH

LOZELLS

FORT DUNLOP

NECHELLS

TO DUDLEY

SOHO

WASHWOOD HEATH

ALUM ROCK

STECHFORD

HAGLEY ROAD

YARDLEY

BOLTON ROAD

LEGEND
1. LODGE ROAD
2. LADYWOOD

ACOCKS GREEN

ALCESTER LANES END

HALL GREEN

COTTERIDGE

RUBERY

REDNAL

O n 7 July 1936 the council had decided that all unprofitable tram routes should be converted, but the war had given Birmingham's 3ft 6in trams a reprieve — although the Aston-Witton section had been converted in 1941 whilst 41 trams had been destroyed by enemy action including 18 in Miller Street in April 1941 and a further four at Washwood Heath — but the fleet had not received much attention and much of the track was in a poor condition. Following the pre-war conversions, most of the routes to the west of the city and many of those to the east had been replaced, primarily by bus, but a significant network to the north and south remained, operated by some 500 trams.

As the end neared, the policy of tramway abandonment was reconfirmed. The fleet was reduced during early 1945 by the scrapping of a number of trams, withdrawn in 1939, that had been retained during the war as 'spares' in case of emergency but never restored to service. In early 1946, permission to convert the Lodge Road, Ladywood and Stechford routes — for which approval had originally been given on 10 January 1939 but deferred due to the war — was sought; authorisation was given by the Ministry of War Transport to convert the Lodge Road and Ladywood routes. It was indicative of things to come when buses were allocated to Washwood Heath depot for the first time in August.

The first route to be converted post-war was that to Lodge Road with its steep grades and sharp curves, which was replaced by buses on 30 March 1947. On 1 April 1947, the Transport Committee agreed to purchase an additional 35 buses to permit the conversion of the Stechford route. This was followed on 30 August 1947 by the conversion of the Ladywood route. These closures allowed for Rosebery Street depot to cease accommodating trams and the closure of the section of track along Dudley Road that had been retained since 1939 solely for depot access.

As at 31 March 1948, Birmingham still operated 440 trams; this was down from 462 two years earlier. The number was to be reduced further when, on 2 October 1948, the four routes serving the Bordesley Green/Stechford corridor were converted to bus operation. By 31 March 1948, the tram fleet had declined to 412. On 5 July 1948, the council decided that all surviving tram routes — plus the city's small trolleybus network — should be converted to bus operation. The trams were scheduled to be replaced in five stages between October 1949 and July 1953; the sixth stage — scheduled for July 1951 — would see the trolleybuses replaced.

The first phase of this conversion programme occurred on 1 October 1949 when the Balsall Heath, Kings Heath and Moseley group of services were converted. These withdrawals resulted in the closure of Moseley Road as a tram shed and the demise of the unusual air-oil brake that was fitted to many of the fleet; the special slipper brakes were required as a result of the steep hill. The second stage saw the services to Witton and Perry Barr operate for the last time on 31 December 1949. Withdrawals following this conversion included the last two of the trams inherited from the City of Birmingham Tramways Co.

By 31 March 1950 the tram fleet had declined to 329 trams. On 22 July 1950, the general manager, Arthur C. Baker (who had held the post since 1928), died; he was replaced by Wilfred Harry Smith on 9 December. By this date, the tramway

Nos 358 and 322 are amongst four trams pictured at the Stechford terminus on 28 March 1948; by this date the Stechford service was nearing the end — it was converted to bus operation on 3 October 1948. *Ian L. Wright/Online Transport Archive*

October 1950 was to see the conversion of a number of routes; the casualties were services to Lozells, Saltley, Washwood Heath and Alum Rock. Routes 8 and 10 were equipped for the operation of bow collectors. Unusually for a 3ft 6in gauge tramway, Birmingham was permitted to operate fully-enclosed tramcars. Pictured at the Alum Rock terminus of route 8 is No 802. *Phil Tatt/ Online Transport Archive*

system had further contracted with the conversion on 30 September of the routes serving Lozells and Saltley. These conversions saw the end of Washwood Heath and Witton depots as tram sheds. Amongst the trams withdrawn at this stage was No 395; this was identified as a candidate for preservation and used after withdrawal as a works shunter at Kyotts Lake Road before being passed to the Birmingham Museum of Science & Industry in June 1953.

By 31 March 1951, the tram fleet had almost halved since the end of the Second World War, being reduced to 263; this number was not to decrease significantly during the year as 1951 was to see the final elimination of the city's trolleybus routes — on 30 June — rather than any further tramway conversions. As a result, the tram fleet was 256 strong at 31 March 1952. However, this stability was not to last long as, on 5 July 1952, the penultimate stage of the conversion programme saw the elimination of trams on the busy Bristol Road corridor. This included the long routes out to Rubery, Rednal and Cotteridge. These conversions resulted in the withdrawal of more than 100 trams, including the last air-braked trams and the end of trams being allocated to Cotteridge (routes 36, 46 and 53) and Selly Oak (routes 35, 54, 69-72) depots.

The results of the 1952 conversions saw the tram fleet reduced to 120 by 31 March 1953. The final stage of the conversion programme occurred on 4 July 1953 with the demise of the surviving routes to Erdington, Short Heath, Pype Hayes and Fort Dunlop. The official last tram was No 616, which was 'decorated' with graffiti-style lettering (in a form that had been trialled on withdrawn No 710 at Kyotts Lake Road Works prior to its adoption). A number of trams were moved to Witton Lane depot as they came out of public service; later

that day the remaining trams in Miller Street were moved under their own power to Kyotts Lake Road; a short gap in the overhead between High Street and Moor Street required them to coast and any that failed were given a gentle shunt by a breakdown lorry.

Following the closure, all the surviving trams were eventually scrapped at Kyotts Lake Road, with the last being disposed by the end of August 1953. The last tram scrapped was railgrinder No 8 (ex-No 226) which was the only tram — other than preserved No 395 — extant on 8 August 1953.

DEPOTS

The Birmingham system had shrunk considerably pre-war, with the result that a number of depots used by the corporation had closed by 1940. These were Birchfield Road (closed 3 October 1924), Bournbrook (11 July 1927), Albion (2 April 1939), Highgate Road (5 January 1937), Hockley

(1 April 1939), Silver Street (31 March 1912), Smethwick (30 September 1939) and Yardley (1 January 1912). This left eight operational depots plus the main workshops — Kyotts Lake Road — operational into the post-war era. These were as follows.

Cotteridge depot was originally opened by the City of Birmingham Tramways Co Ltd on 23 June 1904 and passed to the corporation on 1 July 1911. It closed to trams in July 1952 with the conversion of the Bristol Road and Pershore Road group of routes.

Coventry Road depot was opened by the corporation on 24 November 1906. It was to survive until the conversion of the Stechford routes in October 1948.

Miller Street was the only operational depot that survived through to the final closure of the Birmingham system in July 1953; it had originally been opened by the corporation on 4 January 1904.

Moseley Road was opened by the corporation on 1 January 1907; it survived

The longest tram routes in Birmingham were those that stretched out along the Bristol Road to Longbridge, Rubery and Rednal along with the associated services along the Pershore Road. These routes were all converted to bus operation on 6 July 1952. The Rednal terminus, at which No 809 is pictured on route 70, was heavily used by those seeking to gain access to the Lickey Hills and was provided with substantial cast-iron shelters to protect passengers awaiting their trams back to the city. *Phil Tatt/Online Transport Archive*

One of the routes to survive through until final closure on 4 July 1953 was Pype Hayes Park; here No 683, one of a number of Brush-built trams delivered between 1924 and 1929, is pictured at the terminus. Note the Burnley Clock to regulate time-keeping and the ornate shelter. *F. E. J. Ward/Online Transport Archive*

through until the conversion of the Moseley routes in October 1947.

The conversion of the Ladywood routes in August 1947 saw the first depot closure in Birmingham post-war with the demise of Rosebery Street; this had originally been opened by the corporation on 14 April 1906.

The last new tram depot to be opened by the corporation, on 12 July 1927, was Selly Oak; this was to survive through until July 1952 and the conversion of the Bristol Road and Pershore Road routes.

Two depots were to close in September 1950. Washwood Heath originally dated to 2 May 1907 when it was opened by the corporation; Witton Lane, however, dated back originally to 26 December 1882 when it was opened by the Birmingham & Aston Tramways Co Ltd. It passed, via the City of Birmingham Tramways Co Ltd, to the

corporation on 1 January 1912. Although closed as a running shed, Witton Lane continued to receive withdrawn trams through to the system's final closure in July 1953, with a considerable number being scrapped there. Following final closure it was used, until the collection's transfer to Aldridge in 2011, as the Aston Manor Road Transport Museum.

The corporation's main workshops were located at Kyotts Lake Road. This had originally been opened as a depot by the Birmingham Central Tramway Co Ltd in February 1885. It passed, via the City of Birmingham Tramways Co Ltd, to the corporation on 1 July 1906. Thereafter ceasing to be an operational depot — except for a brief period in 1907 — the building was rebuilt as the main works in which guise it served the trams through to final closure.

CLOSURES

30 March 1947	32 — Lodge Road
30 August 1947	33 — Ladywood
2 October 1948	11 — City to Bordesley Green via Fazeley Street; 12 — City to Bordesley Green via Deritend; 84 — City to Stechford via Deritend; 90 — City to Stechford via Fazeley Street
1 October 1949	37 — City to Cannon Street; 38 — City to Kings Heath via Balsall Heath; 39 — City to Alcester Lanes End via Balsall Heath; 40 — City to Kings Heath via Leopold Street; 41 — City to Trafalgar Road via Leopold Street; 42 — City to Alcester Lanes End via Bradford Street; 48 — City to Kings Heath via Bradford Street; 50 — Albert Street to Trafalgar Road via Bradford Street; 65 — City to Moseley Village via Leopold Street; 66 — City to Moseley Village via Balsall Heath; 67 — City to Moseley Village via Bradford Street
31 December 1949	3X — City to Witton via Aston Cross; 6 — City to Perry Barr
30 September 1950	5 — Lozells to Gravelly Hill; 8 — City to Alum Rock; 9 — City to Ward End (Sladefield Road); 10 — City to Washwood Heath
6 July 1952	35 — City to Selly Oak; 36 — City to Cotteridge; 46 — City to British Oak; 53 — City to Dogpool; 54 — City to Priory Road; 69 — City to Northfield; 70 — City to Rednal; 71 — City to Rubery; 72 — City to Longbridge
4 July 1953	1 — City to Stockland Green; 2 — City to Erdington; 63 — City to Tyburn Road; 64 — City to High Street, Erdington; 78 — City to Short Heath; 79 — City to Pype Hayes Park

FLEET

3, 8, 13/17/18, 20

These were the surviving cars from the original batch of twenty supplied to the corporation by ERTCW in 1904. Fitted with Brill 22E maximum traction bogies, Nos 1-10 were fitted with balcony top covers supplied by Milnes Voss in 1905 whilst Nos 11-20 received UEC balcony top covers two years later. Nos 4, 9, 10 and

Birmingham No 13 was one of six survivors of a batch of 20 trams that had originally been new in 1904; it was to survive in service until early 1950. *F. N. T. Lloyd-Jones/ Online Transport Archive*

16 received Burnley-type bogies supplied by Brush during late 1923 and early 1924, with the rest of the batch receiving similar bogies supplied by EMB between late 1923 and mid-1925. Between January 1924 and December 1929, all cars were fitted with platform vestibules and modified staircases. No 19 was damaged by German bombing in Witton depot in December 1940, whilst Nos 1, 2, 4, 5-7, 10, 11 and 14 were destroyed by enemy action in April 1941 when housed at Miller Street depot with Nos 9, 12 and 15 damaged. Nos 9, 12, 15 and 19 were never to return to service, being eventually scrapped in June 1945. Of the remaining six cars, No 8 was withdrawn in October 1949 with the last five succumbing between January and March the following year.

49, 50/53/55/59, 61/63/64/67, 222/44/48/54-56/59/60/62

These 18 trams were survivors of the 'Brill' class that dated originally to 1905. During

1905 and 1906 UEC supplied 50 open-top cars — Nos 21-70. These were followed by a further 80 open-top cars delivered from the same manufacturer during 1907 and 1908 — Nos 221-300. All were fitted with Brill 21E trucks and, following the introduction of the lowbridge 301 type, were fitted with open-balcony top covers between January 1911 and March 1925. The majority — but not Nos 23/24/29, 30/32, 224/27/31/33/41/42/47/57/58/66/71/ 72/74/78/86/88/90-92/95/99, 300 — were also fitted with platform vestibules between June 1923 and October 1928. A number of the class — Nos 55-61/63/64/68, 222/37/52/54/61 — were fitted with bow collectors in 1924 for use on the Lodge Road route; these were the first trams so equipped in the city. Nos 54 and 65 were also to be so fitted in 1927. No 266 was used as an illuminated car from 1909; in March 1930 its body was used to replace that on works car No PW8. This was the first casualty from the 130

Two of the 'Brill' class — Nos 262 and 61 — are pictured on the Lodge Road route shortly before its conversion in March 1947. Their short wheelbase made them ideal for a route that comprised a number of severe curves. *F. N. T. Lloyd-Jones/Online Transport Archive*

trams built. Withdrawals commenced in 1930 with the surviving 27 trams not fitted with platform vestibules being taken out of service between then and early 1932. Withdrawal of the remainder of the type commenced in April 1932 and by the end of the decade, 18 remained extant based at Roseberry Street depot. A number of those withdrawn during this period were sold to Dover and Merthyr Tydfil for further service. These had been retained for operation on the Lodge Road route; the survival of this route, with its sharp curves (for which the 6ft 0in wheelbase 21E trucks were ideal) meant that the survivors lasted through the war. No 63 had been used as an illuminated car prior to 1939; it was stripped of equipment in 1940 although it was not finally scrapped until June 1946. The next casualties were Nos 49 and 254

in January 1946; the remaining 15 trams were all withdrawn and scrapped after the conversion of the Lodge Road route on 30 March 1947.

73, 87/89, 97/99, 104/09/11/13/16/25/37/42/ 44/60/70/72/76/77/83, 207/10

A batch of 150 open balcony cars, Nos 71-220, was supplied by UEC between August 1906 and March 1907. When new, all were fitted with M&G radial four-wheel trucks. The trams had originally been ordered as open-top, but this was amended following a change in January 1906 that permitted the operation of top-covered trams over Birmingham's 3ft 6in gauge network. The radial trucks proved less than successful and a number of cars saw modification or replacement. By 1928, all were fitted with Brush-built

No 89 — seen here in a pre-war view on route 29 to Bearwood — was one of 22 of the batch that were stored during the war in case of emergency; all were sold for scrap in June 1945 without ever operating after 1939. *W. A. Camwell/ NTM*

Pictured outside
Washwood Heath
depot is No 357;
this was one of the
surviving trams from
a batch of 100 built
by UEC in 1911. This
was one of 11 of the
batch restored to
service during the
war to maintain
services; it was to
survive until the
closure of Washwood
Heath depot in
October 1950. *F. N.
T. Lloyd-Jones/Online
Transport Archive*

Peckham P35s with the exceptions of
Nos 82, 101/46/52/63 and 215 that had
UEC flexible axle trucks and Nos 89,
115/25/57/58/61/68/73 and 208 that
were fitted with Brush 8ft 6in trucks. Nos
82, 115/57/58/68 and 208 were fitted
with Conaty trucks from withdrawn
ex-company cars Nos 497/96/94/99, 500
and 495 respectively during December
1936 and January 1937. At the same
time, the Peckham P35 under No 71 was
exchanged for the Brush 8ft 6in truck
under No 161 as No 71 was scheduled for
withdrawal.

The first withdrawal occurred in
January 1937 with the demise of No 71.
The next two casualties were Nos 119
and 202 succumbed in May 1938 and,

by the end of September 1939, all of the
type had been withdrawn from service.
However, 22 had not been scrapped by
the end of December 1939 and these were
retained during the period of the Second
World War in store at Moseley Road
(Nos 111/13/16) and Rosebery Street
(remainder) depots having been restored
to an operational condition. In the event,
other cars were used in place of those
damaged during the war and these 22 cars
saw no further service. They were sold for
scrap in June 1945 to Grahamsleys with
some of the equipment sold for reuse on
the Llandudno & Colwyn Bay.

301/02/04-06/08-22/25-34/36/37/39-45/47/ 49-59/61/63-83/85-89/93-97, 400

With the forthcoming takeover of the
City of Birmingham Tramways Co routes,
100 open-balcony trams were ordered in
two batches from UEC on UEC flexible
trucks. These trams entered service
between November 1911 and February
1912. The trucks proved problematic and
required modification. Between August
1914 and July 1915 No 361 operated with
Burnley bogies whilst No 346 received a
Peckham P22 truck in June 1917. Between
1917 and 1923 five of the batch — Nos
361/67/68/75/79 — operated as single-
deck; replacement open-balcony top covers
were fitted in 1923. The first withdrawal,
No 323, occurred following an accident
in May 1932; another accident victim was
No 335 withdrawn after a collision in
November 1938. No 391 was withdrawn
in April 1939 whilst No 346 followed two
months later; five — Nos 303/07/24/60/90
— were destroyed in Witton depot
following a German raid in December
1940. No 362 was withdrawn the same
month. No 398 was withdrawn following
an accident in January 1941 to be followed
by No 338 in May 1941. No 392 was
withdrawn in November 1943; its body
was transferred to replace that of No 393
in November 1945. Nos 348 and 384 were
withdrawn in September and November
1944 respectively. Conversely, Nos 315/17/

37/44/55/57/63/68/71/79/81, which had been stored in Rosebery Street, were restored to service during 1941. The remains of those cars withdrawn during the war were scrapped during the summer of 1945. Post-war the first withdrawals — Nos 304/19/45/52/53 — occurred following the conversion of the Ladywood route in August 1947. By February 1950, only 26 of the type remained in passenger service; these included three — Nos 343/87/96 — that were reinstated early in 1950 to replace trams that had been withdrawn. The remaining trams — Nos 309/20/21/25/42-44/47/57/59/63/67/71/72/74-77/81/82/85/87/91/94/95/99 — were all withdrawn in October 1950 with the conversion of the routes served by Washwood Heath depot. All were scrapped with the exception of No 395 that was retained for preservation. The last surviving operational car of the batch was No 341; this had been used as the illuminated 'Victory' tram in 1945 and was converted into a single-deck supply car in early 1948 (on which duty it replaced

No 361 which was refitted to re-enter passenger service). No 341 was to survive until July 1952.

401-38/40-50

With the expansion of the system, there was a need to acquire additional cars and a batch of 50 open balcony cars was built by UEC on M&G trucks. The trams entered service between August 1912 and March 1913. One of the batch, No 431, was originally delivered as a single-decker; this was used for a period in the corporation's experimental use of trailers but was converted into a conventional double-decker in May 1923. Although most operated with the M&G trucks for their entire life, No 434 operated with a Brush-built truck between 1920 and 1922, No 445 had a Peckham P22 truck for a period and No 447 had Burnley-style bogies between 1919 and 1923. The first withdrawal, No 439, occurred in February 1941, although the car was not actually sold for scrap until June 1945. Ten more, Nos 404/10/11/17/21/28/30/33/44/49, were withdrawn between January 1947

Birmingham No 418 was one of 50 trams supplied by UEC during 1912 and 1913. The majority of the batch — including No 418 — were to survive in service until the conversion of the Moseley Road routes. *F. N. T. Lloyd-Jones/ Online Transport Archive*

Following the acquisition of the routes previously operated by the City of Birmingham Tramways Co Ltd, 61 trams entered the corporation fleet; only two — Nos 451 and 452 — were to survive the Second World War. The latter is seen on route 6 to Perry Barr; the conversion of this route in December 1949 led to its withdrawal. *F. N. T. Lloyd-Jones/Online Transport Archive*

and September 1949. The remaining 39 cars were all withdrawn following the closure of Moseley Road depot and the Moseley routes in October 1949. All were subsequently scrapped.

451/52

In 1911/12, the corporation took over the routes previously operated by the City of Birmingham Tramways Co Ltd when the company's leases expired. A total of 61 cars were acquired by the company, but only two survived into the post-war years. Nos 451/52 were originally City of Birmingham Nos 178/80 and had been built at the company's Kyotts Lake Road works in 1903 as open-top double-deck cars. Originally fitted with Brush equal-wheel bogies, these were replaced by the corporation with Burnley-style maximum traction bogies built at Kyotts Lake Road.

In 1917, both were rebuilt as single-deckers for use with experiments in trailer operation. This was short-lived and No 452 was restored to open-top condition in 1922. No 451 remained in single-deck guise until 1926, when both were fitted with open-balcony top covers. The two cars were withdrawn in December 1949 following the conversion of the route to Perry Barr.

512-24/26-37/39-63/65/66/69-73/76-81/83-86

The last new trams acquired by the corporation before the outbreak of the First World War were a batch of 75 open-balcony cars supplied by UEC between October 1913 and December 1914. Fitted with M&G-built Burnley-type maximum traction bogies, all 75 were fitted with enclosed balconies between May 1926 and September 1931.

In the April 1941 raid that damaged Miller Street depot, Nos 564/67/68/74/75 were destroyed and No 582 was damaged (and not repaired). During the war, Nos 569-73/76-78/80/81/84-86 received replacement EMB bogies from cars that had been damaged by enemy action and subsequently withdrawn; Nos 570 in December 1948 and 583 in October 1948 were also to receive replacement EMB bogies. In November 1941, No 538 was withdrawn after it had overturned at Holloway Head. This was followed by No 525, which was withdrawn after being destroyed by fire at Rednal in December 1944.

All of the cars damaged by enemy action, along with Nos 525/38, were sold for scrap in June 1945. Of the survivors, the first withdrawals occurred during 1950 as the result of the conversion of the Lozells route in October that year (Nos 530/37/39/40/44/45/50/52/53). Further withdrawals occurred in mid-1951 with the demise of Nos 523/85; the top deck from the latter was used to replace that on No 542. Three further cars succumbed in early 1952 — 521/27/36 — but nineteen — Nos 512-20/22/24/26/28/29/31-35 — were to be withdrawn in July 1952 as the result of the closure of Selly Oak depot. Of the surviving thirty-four, three were withdrawn in late 1952/early 1953 — Nos 551/76/77 — leaving thirty-one to be scrapped following the final closure in July 1953 (Nos

No 586 was one of 31 of the 75-strong batch delivered during 1913 and 1914 that were to survive through to the final closure of the system in July 1953. This was one of the batch to have its lower saloon strengthened by replacing the bulkhead window by a plain panel. *R. W. A. Jones/Online Transport Archive*

541-43/45-49/54-63/65/66/69-73/78-80/83/84/86).

587-636

The first cars to be delivered after the First World War were 50 open-balcony trams built by Brush and delivered between March 1920 and March 1921. All were fitted with Brush-built Burnley-style maximum traction bogies and all received enclosed upper-deck vestibules between July 1927 and November 1931. One of the class — No 630 — was briefly fitted with a bow collector between November 1931 and July 1932. Three of the batch — Nos 632-34 — were damaged during the war but were repaired and returned to service.

The first of the type to be withdrawn was No 604, which had sustained accident damage in November 1949. Four further cars — Nos 610/19/21/25 — were also withdrawn following collisions during January and February 1950, but the bulk of withdrawals commenced following the conversions of October 1950 when air-braked cars were transferred to Selly Oak depot to replace them. A total of twenty-six — Nos 588/90-95/98/99, 600-03/05-07/11/12/15/18/24/26/28/29/31/35 — were taken out of service at this stage.

Of the remaining nineteen cars, four — Nos 589/96, 613/30 — were withdrawn between 1951 and early 1952, leaving Nos 587/97, 608/09/14/16/17/20/22/23/27/32-34/36 to soldier on until the final abandonment.

637-61

In 1923/24 the Midland Railway Carriage & Wagon Co Ltd of Washwood Heath supplied a batch of 25 fully-enclosed trams to the corporation; these were the

No 633 was one of a batch of 50 trams delivered during 1920 and 1921; it was one of three of the type damaged during the war. Pictured on Steelhouse Lane, with a route 79 Pype Hayes Park service, No 633 was one of 15 of the type to survive until July 1953. Birmingham had a series of terminal loops fringing the central area with no through running. *R. W. A. Jones/Online Transport Archive*

only trams built by this manufacturer for Birmingham. All were fitted with Burnley-type maximum traction bogies supplied by EMB. This batch of cars spent most of its career allocated to Miller Street depot, where Nos 645/49/57 suffered severe damage during a Luftwaffe raid in April 1941. All were repaired and returned to service. Although it was expected that the class would be retained until the final closure of the system, five of the class — Nos 638/41/43/44/52 — were all taken out of service between late 1952 and early 1953. Apart from No 652, all were victims of accident damage. The remaining twenty trams were all scrapped after the final abandonment.

662/64-68/70/72-79/82-84/86-96/98, 700/01
Built by Brush, these fully-enclosed trams were delivered in two batches: Nos 662-81

in March and April 1924 and Nos 682-701 between December 1924 and February 1925. All were fitted with EMB-built Burnley-style maximum traction bogies. Eight of the cars — Nos 663/69/71/80/81/85/97/99 — were destroyed in April 1941 when Miller Street depot was hit by a German bomb; a number of others, most notably Nos 672/82/84/87/91, were damaged but repaired. As with other all-electric cars, the surviving cars of this batch were retained to operate the last remaining services and 27 remained until the end of the system in July 1953. The five exceptions — Nos 666/75/83/89 and 701 — were all withdrawn between October 1952 and June 1953.

704-06/09/10/12/13/15-17/19/21/22/25/26/28-31
Between September 1925 and January 1926, Brush supplied a batch of 30 fully-enclosed

The locally-based Midland Railway Carriage & Wagon Co supplied 25 trams to the corporation during 1923 and 1924. No 643, pictured here at Erdington, was one of five withdrawn in late 1952/early 1953. *Phil Tatt/Online Transport Archive*

No 682, seen at the Pype Hayes Park terminus, was one of 50 trams built by Brush during 1924 and 1925. It was one of a number of the batch damaged by enemy action during the war; repaired, it was to survive through to the closure of the system in July 1953. *R. W. A. Jones/Online Transport Archive*

Pictured at the Steelhouse Lane terminus of route 79, No 705 was one of 30 fully-enclosed trams delivered during 1925 and 1926. Fourteen of the type, including No 705, survived through to July 1953. Note the pavement stop signs and queue barrier. *Phil Tatt/Online Transport Archive*

cars, Nos 702-31, that were fitted with EMB-built Burnley-style maximum traction bogies. The first withdrawal occurred in March 1940 when No 714 was taken out of service after an accident at the junction of Witton Lane and Park Road. A total of nine cars were withdrawn in December 1940 when the roof of Witton depot collapsed on them as a result of enemy action; the casualties were Nos 702/03/07/08/18/20/23/24/27 and these were followed by No 711, which was severely damaged in April 1941 in the raid on Miller Street depot. A number of other cars of the type, most notably Nos 706/13/15-17/19/21/25/29-31, were also damaged during the war but repaired. The eleven wartime casualties were retained in reserve until sold for scrap in June 1945. As all-electric cars, the survivors were amongst the trams selected to see the Birmingham system through to closure, but five — Nos

709/10/12/15/31 — were all withdrawn during the first six months of 1953, leaving the remainder to soldier on until July 1953 when all were withdrawn for scrap.

732-61

This batch of 30 fully-enclosed cars was built by Brush and delivered during 1926 and 1927. All were fitted with EMB Burnley-style maximum traction bogies. Initially allocated to Rosebery Street for use on the service to Hagley Wood, three — Nos 744/57/59 — were briefly fitted in 1931 with bow collectors for operation on the Washwood Heath routes. This was short-lived, however, and all reverted to trolleypoles the following year. With the conversion of Hagley Road in 1930, the batch was transferred to Cotteridge and Selly Oak depots. The first casualty was No 757, which was taken out of service in

One of the 30 fully-enclosed trams supplied by Brush during 1926 and 1927 is seen at the Rubery terminus of route 71 with its ornate tram shelter. No 741 was one of seven of the batch withdrawn during the first half of 1952. *Phil Tatt/ Online transport Archive*

August 1951 and converted into a cleaners' office at Selly Oak. During early and mid-1952, Nos 740/41/45/47/49/50/55 were all taken out of service for various reasons. The surviving 22 cars were all withdrawn for scrap in July 1952.

762-84/86-811

This batch of air-braked 50 double-deck bogie cars was supplied by Brush on EMB Burnley maximum traction bogies. The necessity of acquiring new trams was the result of the acquisition of 6½ route miles from the Birmingham Power & Traction Co from Dudley/Oldbury to Edmund Street via Smethwick and the need to replace older cars in the fleet. Nos 762-811 were used to displace older cars that were transferred to the ex-company routes. The cars entered service between September 1928 and February 1929 and were fitted with Fischer bow collectors from new.

During the Second World War, Nos 764/81/82/85/86/88/89 and 805 were damaged by enemy action; No 785 was not repaired but was sold for scrap early in 1945. Between July and September 1950, Nos 766/72/97/98 and 808 were converted from bow collector to trolley pole and the remaining 44 were so converted in October 1950 following the conversion of the Washwood Heath routes. All 49 were withdrawn in July 1952 following the conversion of the routes served by Cotteridge and Selly Oak depots. Sold to W.T. Bird & Sons, all were subsequently scrapped at Witton depot.

812-20/22-41

In 1928-29, Short Brothers supplied a batch of 30 fully enclosed trams to the corporation. Short manufactured the bodies on frames supplied by Brush. The Burnley maximum traction bogies were supplied by

No 781 was one of 50 air-braked trams built by Brush and delivered during 1928 and 1929; shown with a bow collector, as originally supplied, all were converted to trolleypole operation by the end of October 1950. All the post-war survivors were withdrawn in July 1952. *Phil Tatt/ Online Transport Archive*

M&T. These were the first tramcars built by the Kent-based company and No 740 was sent to Rochester to enable the company to undertake the work. No 821, the first to be withdrawn, was taken out of service in October 1942 when it was seriously damaged in an accident when it overturned, having run down Breedon Hill from the terminus at Cotteridge. Although never returned to service, the car was not actually sold for scrap until June 1945. The next car to succumb was No 814, which was struck by lightning in April 1952 in Bristol Street. Two more, Nos 817 and 841, were also taken out of service by the end of May 1952, with the surviving 26 all being withdrawn after 6

July 1952 with the conversion of the Bristol Road routes. All were scrapped.

842

In the late 1920s, there was considerable interest in the construction of lightweight cars, using aluminium for the bodywork, as this might result in considerable cost savings in operational terms. The first of two lightweight cars, No 842, was constructed by Short Bros and fitted with English Electric-built Burnley-style maximum traction bogies. It entered service in November 1929, based at Cotteridge depot, but was quickly withdrawn for modification as a result of problems with

During 1928 and 1929 Short Brothers supplied 30 fully-enclosed trams; these were the first trams constructed by the Kent-based company and utilised frames supplied by Brush. No 830 was one of 26 of the type withdrawn in July 1952. *Phil Tatt/ Online Transport Archive*

The first of the two lightweight trams, No 842, is pictured at Rednal during an LRTL tour on 7 June 1952; by this date the tram was coming towards the end of its life — it was withdrawn the following month. *John Meredith/Online Transport Archive*

the ventilation in the lower deck. Following two attempts at modification, the car was fully back in service in June 1930. In 1950, the non-standard bogies were replaced by M&T bogies recovered from No 821. No 842, as an air-braked car, was deemed surplus to requirements after the withdrawal of the Bristol Road routes in July 1952 and sold for scrap.

843
Birmingham's second lightweight car, No 843, was destined to be the last new tram to enter service with the corporation. Built by Brush on M&T Burnley-style maximum traction bogies, the car entered service in September 1930, being based,

like No 842, at Cotteridge depot. The car was to survive until January 1952, when it was sent to Kyotts Lake Road for attention to a defective motor; this fault, and the generally poor condition of the bodywork, resulted in the vehicle being withdrawn at this stage as the costs of repair were considered excessive for a tram scheduled for withdrawal in July 1952 with the abandonment of the Bristol Road routes.

WORKS TRAMS
As with any significant system, Birmingham possessed a number of specialist works cars. However, most had succumbed before the Second World War.

Pictured during a tour of the system on 18 April 1948, No 843 was the last new tram delivered to Birmingham; scheduled for withdrawal in July 1952, it was actually taken out of service earlier in the year with a defective motor. *R. B. Parr/NTM*

The survivors post-war are described in the following paragraphs.

Overhead car No 01 was one of two from a batch of six delivered in 1907 on M&G-built Brill 21E trucks. Converted into a tower wagon in 1924, when it was renumbered from No 4, it was to continue in use through until March 1952. The second of the 1907 batch was stores van No 6; this was, however, withdrawn

Works car No 01 was one of six supplied in January 1907; originally No 4 it was rebuilt as a tower wagon in August 1924 and renumbered 01. It was to survive in service until March 1952. *F. E. J. Ward/ Online Transport Archive*

No PW8 was one of a number of works cars rebuilt from withdrawn passenger cars. It was converted in 1929 when the lower deck of No 266 was combined with the Conaty truck that had previously operated under No 505. Used to shunt trams awaiting scrapping, No PW8 was destined to become the last Birmingham tram scrapped.
F. N. T. Lloyd-Jones/ Online Transport Archive

following the closure of Hockley depot in 1939 but was not scrapped until June 1945. Van No 5 was constructed at Kyotts Lake Road on a Brill 21E truck; it survived until being scrapped in August 1949. Van No 10 was again built at Kyotts Lake Road on a Brill 21E truck, being completed in April 1918. Again effectively withdrawn with the demise of Hockley depot, it saw limited use during the war and was to survive until being sold to George Cohen & Sons in August 1949; it was broken up the following February.

Nos PW8-10 were all converted from passenger cars, having been cut-down to single deck. No PW8 was originally No 505 and was modified in December 1920 when it was fitted with a Conaty truck; its body was scrapped in November 1929 and replaced with that from No 266. Repainted post-war, No PW8 was to survive to become the last Birmingham tram to be scrapped, being used for shunting other scrap trams at Kyotts Lake Road before meeting its

own fate. No PW9 was rebuilt from No 507, again on a Conaty truck, in August 1921; the body was also replaced, with that from No 509, in 1928. No PW9 was to survive until sold for scrap in March 1952. The last of the trio was converted from No 508 in November 1921; again mounted on a Conaty truck, No PW10 was to survive until sold for scrap in June 1945; it was finally dismantled in September 1946. No PW16 was the only survivor of four welding vans; built in October 1920 and fitted with a Brill 21E truck, the tram and its associated trailer saw only limited service after 1945 and both were sold for scrap in June 1945.

After the war, No 341, which had been converted for use as a single-deck illuminated car to mark 'Victory' in March 1945, was rebuilt in 1948 to replace No 361 as a stores car; the latter, used as a stores car since 1939, was restored to passenger service. No 341 was to survive until March 1952 and was subsequently scrapped at Witton depot.

GRIMSBY & IMMINGHAM

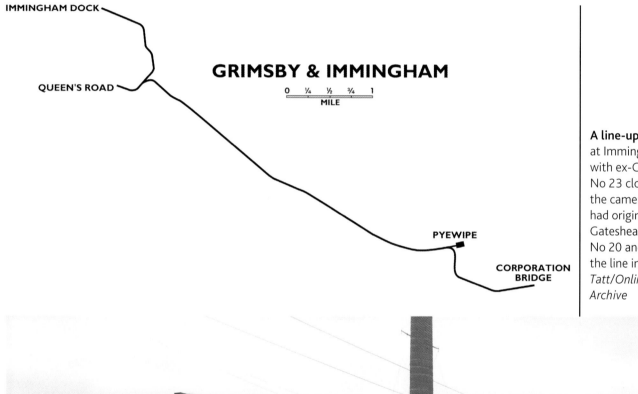

IMMINGHAM DOCK

QUEEN'S ROAD

GRIMSBY & IMMINGHAM

0 ¼ ½ ¾ 1
MILE

PYEWIPE

CORPORATION
BRIDGE

A line-up of trams at Immingham Dock with ex-Gateshead No 23 closest to the camera. This had originally been Gateshead & District No 20 and arrived on the line in 1951. *Phil Tatt/Online Transport Archive*

The 4ft 8½in Grimsby & Immingham emerged from the Second World War in the ownership of the LNER. The wartime years had seen Grimsby Corporation acquire a large area of land — 200 acres — between the tramway and the coast; as this was developed for industrial purposes post-war, it encouraged increased levels of passenger usage on the line. Unfortunately, however, this was to prove contentious later in the tramway's life as none of the companies established on the new industrial estate were willing to contribute to support the line's finances.

During the war, the overhead was removed from the short section of line to Queens Road; although this had been completed during the First World War, it had never been used. In 1945, the points at Immingham Halt providing access to the now unwired section were removed and the unused track was recovered two years later.

By now a further change of ownership was in sight; following the Transport Act of 1947, which nationalised Britain's railway industry, the tramway — as an asset of the LNER — passed to British Railways (Eastern Region) on 1 January 1948. The ex-Newcastle trams emerged in a new brown livery; it was not until 1951, and a decision by the Railway Executive that all of BR's electric vehicles should adopt a green livery, that the fleet was to be painted green.

Ex-Great Central Railway No 14 pictured at Immingham Town in the all-over green livery adopted by British Railways for the Grimsby & Immingham stock. This tram was to be preserved on closure — the only one of the ex-GCR cars to survive. *Derek Norman/Online Transport Archive*

As elsewhere, the wartime years had witnessed a paucity of maintenance and there was particular concern about the section of street track along Corporation Road. During 1948 and 1949 there were talks between the corporation and BR over the future of this section; the former was keen to see it eliminated 'in the interests of the safety of traffic and pedestrians' in a view stated by a deputation from the Highway Committee to the Railway Executive in early 1949. BR was willing to sacrifice the section but only if the corporation funded the cost of road reinstatement. With the corporation unwilling to fund the work, an impasse was reached and, with the route now under no immediate threat, some limited relaying was undertaken.

The other issue faced by the line's new owners was lack of capacity; in 1948, partly as a result of the new industrial development, the line carried 1.35 million passengers. This was initially resolved by the purchase of three single-deck trams — Nos 29, 42 and 77 — from Newcastle Corporation in 1948; these became Grimsby & Immingham Nos 6-8 respectively, but were destined to have a short life on Humberside, all being withdrawn by the end of 1954.

The fleet was further supplemented in 1951 by the purchase of 19 single-deck trams from Gateshead & District. Following refurbishment at York works, which included the reprofiling of the tyres and the addition of a second lamp, the trams were delivered to Pyewipe depot. Of the 19, only 17 entered passenger service; one — ex-Gateshead No 17 — was used as a works car, whilst the nineteenth — ex-Gateshead No 4 — was written off when a crane fell on it during delivery.

Pictured on Corporation Road is ex-GCR No 15; the section of the route from Corporation Bridge along Corporation Road to Cleveland Bridge was to be replaced by corporation-operated buses on 30 June 1956. *Phil Tatt/Online Transport Archive*

The arrival of the ex-Gateshead trams was necessary as a result of the growth in local industries; a total of 19 trams were required to operate the peak hour services with convoys of up to seven trams being deployed to cater for the passenger traffic. Unusually, the line operated round the clock although the frequency was reduced during off-peak hours and overnight.

In February 1955, the clerk to Grimsby Rural District Council told members of the council that 1955 was one of the years in which the council was empowered to acquire the street tramway section to Corporation Bridge. On 30 June 1955, BR told the council that the route would be available, free of charge, provided that the Grimsby Corporation provided a replacement bus service; the offer was accepted and six second-hand buses were acquired. Despite opposition,the single track section of line from Cleveland Bridge to Corporation Bridge was withdrawn on 30 June 1956, with the replacement buses connecting with the curtailed tram service at Cleveland Bridge. No withdrawals occurred at this time as passenger traffic over the remaining section of the route was still substantial; indeed, there were still in excess of 1 million passenger journeys in 1956.

The following January saw Nos 1 and 14 involved in a fatal accident however, both trams were repaired and restored to service. Later in 1957, the power station at Immingham Dock was reduced to stand-by status with power obtained generally from the grid; it was to close completely in 1958.

It was in 1958 that the question of the future of the remainder of the line emerged. As a result of its history, a significant number of passengers travelled free of charge and requests for financial support from the recently established industries fell on deaf ears. As a result, BR applied for permission to close the line in July 1958. At the inquiry into the closure, BR reported that the line's revenue — £23,000 — was significantly less than the £72,000 it cost to operate. The unwillingness of Lincolnshire County Council to construct a new road, and thus the lack of alternative transport facilities, led the local authorities to oppose closure.

At the TUCC meeting held in Grimsby on 24 April 1959 to discuss the closure, a compromise was agreed. Whilst the tramway would be retained only for the peak-hour services, buses would be used in off-peak hours, running via the indirect road. This new arrangement came into effect on 28 September 1959 and reduced the number of trams required to a maximum of ten.

Patronage on the tramway continued to decline — although even at closure it still carried about 250,000 per annum — and, on 29 December 1960, BR again proposed closure. This time, however, BR went further; it announced that if permission to close the line was refused, it would still withdraw the trams and replace them by DMUs. This time, perhaps fearful that the new DMU service might adversely affect revenue on its own bus service to the docks, Grimsby Corporation backed the closure. When the TUCC met for the second time in the line's history, on 21/22 February 1961, there were only ten objections and consent to closure was given. The first day on which the TUCC had permitted closure — 1 July 1961 — was announced as the final day of operation. On the last day, the last car was ex-GCR No 14; this departed from Immingham Dock at 2.12pm suitably decorated and carrying a commemorative headboard.

Following closure, the bulk of the fleet was scrapped although three cars — two of the ex-Gateshead trams (Nos 5 and 10) and ex-GCR No 14 — were preserved as was the tower maintenance trolley.

DEPOT
The Grimsby & Immingham had a single depot/workshop; this was located at Pyewipe and opened with the line on 15 May 1912. It was to survive through to final closure on 1 July 1961. Unusually, the

trams were stored in the open at Pyewipe, entering the building only for routine maintenance purposes. All major work was undertaken at BR workshops.

CLOSURES

30 June 1956   Cleveland Bridge to
                      Corporation Bridge
1 July 1961   Cleveland Bridge to
                      Immingham

FLEET

1-5, 9-16

These cars were the surviving examples of the 16 trams acquired by the Great Central Railway. Nos 1-8 were delivered in 1911, Nos 9-12 in 1913 and Nos 13-16 in 1915. All were built by Brush and fitted with Brush-built equal-wheel bogies. No 5 was one of the batch of Nos 5-8 that had a smaller seating capacity than the remainder of the GC's fleet; this car was retained for works' duties when the other three cars of the batch were withdrawn in 1931. It was eventually replaced by No DE320224. Nos 15 and 16 were rebuilt in the early 1950s following collision damage. Two of the trams were withdrawn in 1951 and two more in 1952, all as the result of accident damage; the remaining eight

Four of the surviving ex-GCR trams — with No 1 at the head — stand at the Corporation Bridge terminus on 21 June 1953. The others are Nos 11, 14 and 5. *John Meredith/Online Transport Archive*

survived until the final closure of the line. One of the cars — No 14 — was secured for preservation; it is now part of the National Tramway Museum collection at Crich.

6-8

In 1948, three second-hand cars were acquired from Newcastle upon Tyne Corporation; originally Nos 29, 42 and 77 respectively on Tyneside, the three were all originally built by Hurst Nelson on Peckham P25 trucks in 1901 and rebuilt by Newcastle Corporation in 1932/33. These were the only trams employed by the Grimsby & Immingham to be fitted with upholstered seats. These three cars were withdrawn in 1954.

17-33

In 1951/52, British Railways took advantage of the demise of Gateshead's tramway system to acquire a number of single-deck cars to supplement the existing fleet. Numbered by Gateshead originally as 57, 18, 9, 5, 56, 7, 20, 3, 6, 10, 16, 58, 1, 8, 11, 60 and 59, the 17 cars were originally built between 1921 and 1928 and were fitted with Brill 39E1 maximum traction bogies under bodies supplied by either Brush (Nos 1, 20, 56-60) or Gateshead & District itself (remainder). Gateshead No 4 was also acquired but this was destroyed in transit and never entered service. The last of the ex-Gateshead trams were withdrawn in 1961. Two — No 5 at Crich and No 10 at Beamish — survive in preservation.

DE320224

A further ex-Gateshead car — No 17 — was also acquired; this was converted into a new works car to replace No 5. Built by Gateshead & District on Brill 39E1 bogies, No DE320224 was to survive until the system's closure in 1961.

One of the three ex-Newcastle trams, No 6 (previously Newcastle No 29) is pictured at Corporation Bridge. These trams were to survive only until 1954. *Peter N. Williams/Online Transport Archive*

A total of 17 ex-Gateshead trams entered passenger service on the Grimsby & Immingham line during 1951 and 1952. No 31 — ex-Gateshead No 11 — is also pictured at the Corporation Bridge terminus. *Phil Tatt/ Online Transport Archive*

An 18th ex-Gateshead car was also used by British Railways; this was ex-No 17 that was converted into a works car and numbered DE320224 in BR's service stock list. It is seen here alongside the line's railborne tower wagon at Pyewipe depot. As the infrastructure declined during the final years, these vehicles were in almost daily use. *R. Stephens/Online Transport Archive*

LEICESTER

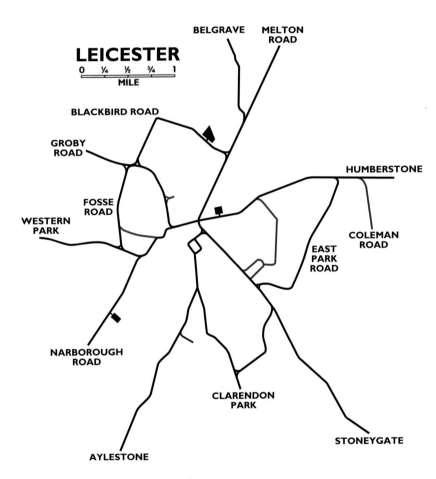

The Second World War had given Leicester's 4ft 8½ in gauge trams a reprieve and the system entered the last year of war relatively unscathed. The only casualty was the withdrawal of No 19 in 1941 as a result of accident damage.

The first conversion was to take place before the end of hostilities when trams were withdrawn from the Clarendon Road via Welford Road section on 1 May 1945. This was a relatively lightly used section and was largely paralleled by the Knighton Road bus route.

The abandonment allowed for the lifting of the track and its reuse elsewhere on the system at a time when obtaining new rail was difficult.

The next conversion occurred on 5 January 1947 and saw trams withdrawn from the Aylestone Road route; again, certain track was lifted for reuse. This was followed on 15 July 1947 by the conversion of the Fosse Road route. Almost 30 trams were withdrawn, including No 76; its body was sold to a private owner. Rescued in August 1960, it was fully restored and now forms part of the NTM collection.

Despite these conversions, the tram still catered for more than half the public transport provision in the city and it was to be almost a further 16 months before the next conversion. This was on 21 November 1948 when trams were withdrawn from the Narborough Road and Western Park (via Hinckley Road) routes. A further 18 trams were withdrawn as a result of these conversions. By this date the fleet had been reduced to 72 trams.

Early 1949 was to see the pace of conversion accelerated with five routes succumbing: Groby Road on 23 January; Clarendon Park and Blackbird Road on 13 March; East Park Road on 15 May; and Melton Road on 3 July. These conversions resulted in the withdrawal of 33 trams, leaving 39 in service. The conversion of the Blackbird Road route resulted in the track being lifted from Leicester's only significant reservation; this was then relaid behind the main depot at Abbey Park Road to facilitate the scrapping of the remaining trams.

Pictured at the Stoneygate terminus is No 152; it is believed that this was the only Leicester tram to have received a repaint post-war. The tram, freshly repainted, was used for a tour of the system by the LRTL on 18 August 1946. The Belgrave to Stoneygate section was converted to bus operation on 9 October 1949. The conversion programme was known as 'Operation Scrap-Iron'.
F. E. J. Ward/Online Transport Archive

...e of the features of all Leicester tram termini was the ...ey reverser; it can be seen clearly here at the terminus on ... East Park Road with No 58 in the foreground and No 143 ...e distance. *F. E. J. Ward/Online Transport Archive*

No 110 is pictured on the reservation at Blackbird Road; this section was abandoned on 13 March 1949 and the track salvaged. No 110 was the last tram in the fleet to operate in the pre-1937 livery; it was to retain this until withdrawal in October 1949. *F. N. T. Lloyd-Jones/Online Transport Archive*

Leicester's last tram route was that to Humberstone — route 8 — which was to be converted to bus on 9 November 1949. Here No 97 is seen at the terminus. *F. N. T. Lloyd-Jones/Online Transport Archive*

The next route to be converted was the sole surviving cross-city service — that linking Stoneygate with Belgrave Road — on 9 October 1949. This conversion saw the demise of a further 21 trams, leaving 15 operational for the final route. The final conversion occurred on 9 November 1949 when trams were withdrawn from the Humberstone service. The official last tram, suitably decorated, was No 58, which conveyed guests to the depot at Abbey Park Road.

In theory, the corporation was due to preserve No 36; however, a dispute between the transport and museum departments resulted in the tram being scrapped on 24 April 1950 — the day before the museum department decided that it could accommodate the tram and asked for its transfer. Fortunately, although No 36 escaped preservation, No 76 was subsequently rescued and, in 2009, a further body, that of No 31, was secured and is currently undergoing restoration.

DEPOTS

Leicester Corporation possessed four depots during the electric era. Two — London Road (opened 18 May 1904) and Narborough Road (opened 17 July 1904) — were both closed in 1922. Humberstone Gate depot was originally opened by the Leicestershire Tramways Co Ltd for horse trams on 24 December 1874. It was taken over by the corporation on 1 July 1901. The last horse trams operated on 31 October 1904 and electric trams took over from the following day. The depot closed with the system on 9 November 1949. Abbey Park Road, where the main workshops were also situated, opened on 18 May 1904; extended in 1915, the depot and works remained operational for the trams until the system's final closure. There was a fifth depot — Thurcaston Road — which opened for the horse trams of the Leicester Tramways Co Ltd in 1888 and, following the take-over by the corporation in 1901, closed in 1904.

CLOSURES

1 May 1945	Clarendon Road via Welford Road
5 January 1947	Aylestone
15 July 1947	Fosse Road
21 November 1948	Narborough Road / Western Park
23 January 1949	Groby Road
13 March 1949	Clarendon Road via Clarendon Park Road / Blackbird Road
15 May 1949	East Park Road
3 July 1949	Melton Road
9 October 1949	Stoneygate to Belgrave
9 November 1949	Humberstone

FLEET

1-9, 11/13-18, 20-23/25-28, 30-33/35-43/ 45-47, 50-52/54-87/89-97/99

During 1903 and 1904, ERTCW supplied no fewer than 99 open-top four-wheel trams. These were all fitted with Brill 21E trucks. All were fitted with balcony tops between 1912 and 1927 and all bar Nos 12, 24, 29 and 44 were rebuilt as fully enclosed between 1924 and 1927. Nos 10, 12, 19, 24, 29, 34, 44, 48, 49, 53, 88 and 98 were withdrawn between 1933 and 1939. In September 1947 No 20 was renumbered 8 and scrapped whilst No 8 was renumbered 162. The post-war survivors were all withdrawn between 1945 and 1949. One of the cars, No 76, was later salvaged for preservation by the Tramway Museum Society and fully restored to open balcony / open vestibule status at Crich; it remains on display at the National Tramway Museum. A second body — that from No 31 — has also survived and is now in the care of the Tram 31 Group with a view to eventual restoration.

101-21

This batch of 21 balcony top cars was delivered in 1905 and was supplied by

No 7 stands at the stub terminus of route 8 to Humberstone at Clock Tower; the depot located at Humberstone Gate was located to the right of the photographer and its access track can be seen in the road alongside the tram. *F. N. T. Lloyd-Jones/ Online Transport Archive*

UEC on Brill 21E four-wheel trucks. All were rebuilt as fully enclosed between 1924 and 1934 and survived until withdrawal between 1945 and 1949.

100/23-27/29-40

In 1905, UEC supplied a batch of 20 open-top cars, Nos 122-41, fitted with Brill 21E trucks. In 1912, No 137 was renumbered 100 and No 141 became No 137. All received open-balcony top covers between 1912 and 1927 and were fully enclosed between 1924 and 1934, with the exception of Nos 122/28; the two unrebuilt cars were both withdrawn

prior to the start of the Second World War. In September 1948, Nos 108 and 115 exchanged numbers with the new No 108 being scrapped; all of the survivors were withdrawn for scrap during the period 1945 to 1949.

141-50

These ten cars were supplied in 1913 by UEC on Brill 21E trucks as open-balcony cars designed for a PAYE operation. All of this batch were also converted to fully enclosed between 1924 and 1934, surviving to be withdrawn between 1945 and 1949.

Passing under the railway line, with the ex-Great Northern Railway Humberstone signalbox and station prominent above it, is No 117 with a service towards Humberstone. This was one of 21 open-balcony trams built originally in 1905 that were converted to fully enclosed between 1924 and 1934. *F. N. T. Lloyd-Jones/Online Transport Archive*

151-60

In 1914, Brush, based in nearby Loughborough, supplied a batch of ten open-balcony trams. These were delivered on Brill 21E trucks and were rebuilt as fully enclosed between 1924 and 1934. All were withdrawn between 1945 and 1949.

161-66

Built in Leicester Corporation's own workshops in 1920, Nos 161-66 were a batch of open-balcony cars fitted with Preston Standard 21E trucks. All were rebuilt as fully enclosed by 1934. In December 1947 No 162 was renumbered 20 and then scrapped. The remainder were all withdrawn between 1945 and 1949.

167-71/73/74/77/78

The last new trams delivered to Leicester Corporation were a batch of 12 open-balcony cars built in 1920 by English Electric on Preston Standard 21E trucks. All were rebuilt as fully enclosed by 1934. Three of the type — Nos 172/75/76 — were withdrawn in 1939 with the remainder surviving to be withdrawn between 1945 and 1949.

179-81

Leicester possessed three works. No 179 was a water car and railgrinder supplied by ERTCW on a Brill 21E truck in 1904. This had originally been numbered 100 when new, becoming No 151 in 1912 and

Pictured on the reserved track section along Blackbird Road — the only reserved track on the system — is No 129; this was one of 20 open-top trams supplied by UEC in 1905. *F. N. T. Lloyd-Jones/Online Transport Archive*

No 150 was the last of a batch of 10 trams delivered in 1913 that were originally designed for PAYE operation; originally open balcony, all 10 were rebuilt as fully enclosed. *F. N. T. Lloyd-Jones/Online Transport Archive*

Again pictured on the Blackbird Road reservation, No 158 was one of a batch of 10 trams built by Brush in 1914; curiously, although Brush was based in neighbouring Loughborough, this was the only batch of trams that this local manufacturer supplied to Leicester Corporation. *F. N. T. Lloyd-Jones/Online Transport Archive*

Seen on route 1 to East Park Road is No 162; this was one of six trams built in the corporation's Abbey Park Road works — the only tram bodies to be completed there. *F. N. T. Lloyd-Jones/ Online Transport Archive*

The highest numbered passenger car in the Leicester fleet was No 178; this was one of 12 built by English Electric and delivered in 1920. *F. N. T. Lloyd-Jones/Online Transport Archive*

179 eight years later. Nos 180/81 were also combined water cars and rail grinders, being supplied by UEC on Brill 21E trucks in 1905 and 1909 respectively. Originally numbered 142/43, they became Nos 152/53 in 1912 and 180/81 in 1920.

Leicester possessed three works cars; No 179 was the oldest, being supplied originally by ERTCW in 1904. Originally No 100, it became No 151 in 1912 and No 179 eight years later. *Barry Cross Collection/Online Transport Archive*

MIDLAND METRO

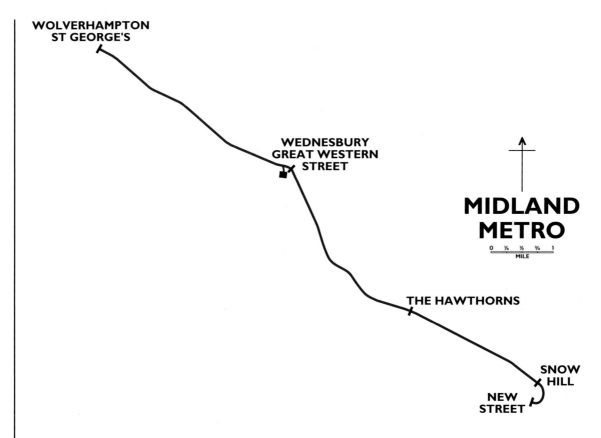

Although there had been proposals for an ambitious light rail network serving the West Midlands in the early 1980s, it was not until the second half of the decade that plans began to become more concrete.

In February 1988, it was announced that the first phase was to be a line between Birmingham and Wolverhampton, utilising in main the largely abandoned trackbed of the ex-Great Western Railway route between Birmingham Snow Hill and Wolverhampton Low Level. A bill seeking powers to construct this and two further routes — from Birmingham city centre to Fiveways and from Wolverhampton to Dudley via Walsall and the Merry Hill shopping centre — was deposited in November 1988 and was enacted on 16 November 1989.

After considerable delays, the contract for the construction and operation of the line was let to the Altram consortium — National Express (who operate the line), Ansaldo-Breda (who built the first batch of trams) and John Laing (the contractors who built the line) — in August 1995. The completion date was originally scheduled to be August 1998, but this was missed by almost a year, resulting in a compensation payment by the consortium. The line is owned by Transport for West Midlands and operation is scheduled to be brought in-house in October 2018.

Opening of the 12½-mile route took place on 31 May 1999. Between Snow Hill and The Hawthorns the line runs parallel to the reopened Network Rail route from Snow Hill to Stourbridge Junction; from the Hawthorns to Priestfield, the line operates over the ex-GWR route and, from Priestfield to Wolverhampton St George's, the line operates in the street. The section through Wolverhampton was the only street section planned in the original Phase 1.

In June 2012, work commenced on the Snow Hill to New Street extension; the first trams operated on the section from Snow Hill to Bull Street on 6 December 2015 and the line was opened throughout on 30 May 2016. Further extensions of the route through to Centenary Square and then to Edgbaston via Fiveways are under development. An extension from Wolverhampton St George's to the railway station was announced in March 2016 and approval of the Transport & Works Order Act was given by the-then Secretary of State for Transport, Patrick McLoughlin, in 2016. It is expected that the Centenary Square and Wolverhampton extensions will

When the Midland Metro first opened, there was only one section of street running, from Priestfield to Wolverhampton. On 20 August 1999 No 16 makes its way towards Wolverhampton under the railway bridges on Bilston Road. The nearer of the two bridges carries the freight-only branch to the local steel terminal; when recorded, the branch was still provided with 25kV catenary; this has been subsequently removed. *Les Folkard/Online Transport Archive*

On 30 August 1999 Midland Metro No 13 is pictured at Snow Hill station; the short section serving the station was to close with the opening of the extension to Bull Street on 6 December 2015. *Author*

million towards the cost. The new 2km long line will include five stops.

There are further long-term plans for the extension of the network to Adderley Street via Moor Street and Curzon Street (to serve the station planned to serve the proposed HS2 link to London) and for the route south from Wednesbury to Stourbridge Junction via Merry Hill. Limited work on the latter commenced in early 2017 although reuse of this line is linked to Network Rail's desire to see the Walsall to Stourbridge Junction line, closed in 1993, reopened for freight traffic. At the present time, these two extensions are scheduled for the early years of the next decade. Longer term plans envisage the extension of the line to Adderley Park through to Coventry.

DEPOT
The Midland Metro possesses a single depot and workshop; this is situated at Wednesbury, on the south side of the running line, and opened with the route on 30 May 1999.

OPENING DATES

30 May 1999	Birmingham Snow Hill to Wolverhampton St George's
6 December 2015	Birmingham Snow Hill to Bull Street
30 May 2016	Bull Street to Birmingham New Street
2019	Birmingham New Street to Centenary Square
2019	Wolverhampton St George's to Wolverhampton railway station
Post-2019	Centenary Square to Edgbaston

FLEET

1-16
The original fleet that operated over the Midland Metro was built by

be opened in 2019, whilst that to Edgbaston will follow early in the next decade. Work formally started on the Centenary Square and Edgbaston — the Westside Extension — in early September 2017 with the temporary removal of Anthony Gormley's Iron Man statue from Victoria Square; this was done following the announcement on 1 September 2017 that funding for the £149 million project was in place with the government providing £9.8

Ansaldo-Breda of Naples in Italy. Designated T-69, the 16 trams, Nos 1-16, were built between 1996 and 1999 and entered service with the line's opening on 30 May 1999. Built as articulated single-deckers, the T-69 cars had a capacity of 156 (56 seated with 100 standing). In order to continue to operate alongside the newer Urbos 3 trams, which are wider, the T-69s were modified with wider steps so that they were compatible with the narrower platforms. All were refurbished during 2013 to achieve this; other work done at this stage included the replacement of the traditional blinds with LED displays. The last of the T-69s were withdrawn during August 2015, although they were initially retained in store at Long Marston pending possible reuse once the network was extended. However, in early 2018 the T-69s were auctioned off, with all bar three being sold for scrap. Of the remaining three, No 7 has been donated to UK Tram whilst No 11 is to become a museum exhibit in Birmingham. No 16 remains out of use with the operator.

17-37

Built by CAF of Beasain in Spain, Nos 17-37 are single-deck articulated Urbos 3 trams with a capacity of 210 passengers (54 seated and 156 standing). Built from 2012 onwards, the first of the type entered service on the Midland Metro on 5 September 2014. By the late summer of 2015, they had completely replaced the original fleet. Being slightly wider than the original units, the new trams required the existing platforms to be modified slightly before they could enter service.

The section of line from Bull Street to the new terminus at New Street station opened on 30 May 2016. On 28 December 2016 one of the new AF-built trams, No 366, descends towards Stephenson Street. *Paul Collins*

Prior to their introduction to service, the 16 Ansaldo-built trams were tested at the Midland Metro's depot at Wednesbury as seen in this view of 3 May 1998; it would be more than a year before passenger services were finally introduced. *Author*

To replace the original rolling stock, Midland Metro acquired 21 Urbos 3 articulated trams from CAF in Spain. No 29 is seen here at the current terminus of the route in Birmingham on Stephenson Street on 30 May 2016. Work has now commenced on the western extension of the system; in connection with this, the CAF-built trams are being modified to enable them to run without overhead through Centenary Square. *Paul Collins*

NOTTINGHAM EXPRESS TRANSIT

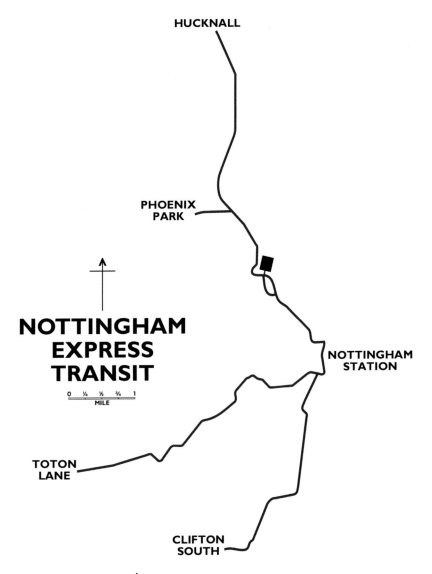

HUCKNALL

PHOENIX
PARK

NOTTINGHAM
STATION

**NOTTINGHAM
EXPRESS
TRANSIT**

0   ¼   ½   ¾   1
MILE

TOTON
LANE

CLIFTON
SOUTH

Although the city's first generation tramway was a relatively early casualty, by the late 1980s the concept of a new tramway — to ease congestion and aid urban regeneration — was actively pursued. Following an announcement in 1998 by the government

that funding for the project was available, in March 2000 the system's promoters — Nottinghamshire County Council and Nottingham City Council — awarded the contract to build, maintain and operate the line to a consortium, Arrow Light Rail Ltd (comprising Adtranz, the builder of the trams, Carillion, responsible for construction, and Transdev with Nottingham City Transport, responsible for operation).

The first phase of the system — from Station Street to Hucknall with a branch to Phoenix Park — opened on 9 May 2004. The network was about 8¾ route miles and had cost some £200 million to complete but even before the first phase was opened, consideration was being given to extending the line. Initial approval for the next phase was given on 5 October 2006 with the final go-ahead following on 30 March 2009; however, before work could commence, Nottinghamshire County Council decided that it could no longer fund its part although it would not block the project if funding could be found. The City Council agreed to take on the additional funding and the entire financial package was approved by the government on 31 July 2009. Despite the arrival of the coalition government in 2010 and its spending review, the project retained its funding.

Although the original consortium bid for the new extension, a second consortium — Tramlink Nottingham — was successful; as a consequence, operation of the new line (plus that of the original section) passed to the new consortium's

NET No 213 is seen in Royal Square on 19 May 2004 with a service heading to the-then terminus at Station Street. *Les Folkard/Online Transport Archive*

participants — Keolis and Wellglade (owner of Trent Barton) — with the involvement of Nottingham City Transport ceasing.

Work started on the construction of the extension in 2012 but was to run late. Track laying was completed on 11 December 2014 and the first section of the new line — from the original terminus on Station Street to Nottingham station — opened on 27 July 2015 and throughout to Clifton South and Chilwell on 25 August 2015. The result of the second phase

NET No 227 on the street section south of Nottingham station; as with all NET trams, this carries a name — *Sir Peter Mansfield. Paul Collins*

was to extend the network to 20 route miles operated by a fleet of 37. There are proposals for further extensions, in particular a link westwards to Derby to provide a connection into the proposed HS2 station at Toton.

DEPOT

The fleet is currently housed at a single depot — Wilkinson Street — to the north of the city centre, which opened with the system in March 2004.

OPENING DATES

9 March 2004	Station Street to Hucknall/Phoenix Park
27 July 2015	Station Street to Nottingham station
25 August 2015	Nottingham station to Clifton South/Chilwell

One of the original batch of 15 Bombardier-built articulated trams, No 207 stands at the Hucknall terminus on 31 May 2004. *Les Folkard/Online Transport Archive*

FLEET

201-15

The fleet's first 15 articulated single-deck trams were built by Bombardier Transportation at Derby. Designated Incentro AT6/5, the design was based around a model produced for Nantes in France. Built in 2002/03 and refurbished in 2013, the 15 trams entered service with the opening of the first phase of the NET system on 9 March 2004.

216-37

For the second phase of the NET system, a batch of 22 Citadis 302 was ordered from the French manufacturer Alstom. The single-deck articulated trams were delivered during 2013 and 2014, with services commencing over NET phase 2 during the summer of 2015.

The second batch of NET trams were 22 — Nos 216-37 — that were supplied by Alstom between September 2013 and November 2014. One of the batch is recorded turning from Victoria Street with a service for Station Street. *Paul Collins*

On 15 April 2004 No 204 heads southbound at Highbury Vale with a service to Station Street. NET at this point runs parallel to the Network Rail 'Robin Hood' line from Nottingham to Mansfield and Worksop. *Les Folkard/ Online Transport Archive*

PLYMOUTH

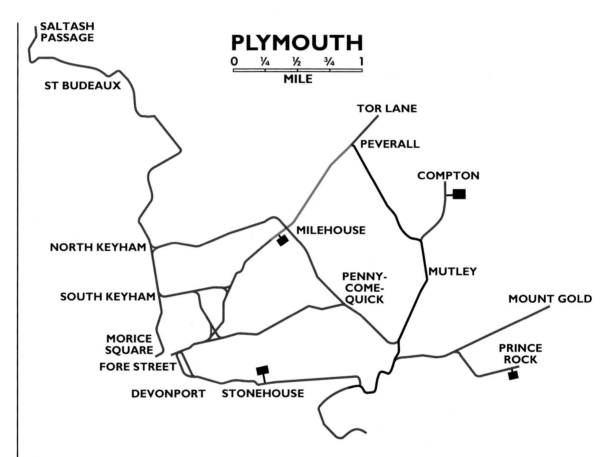

Plymouth Corporation had been pursuing a policy of tramcar conversion prior to the outbreak of war in September 1939; the first conversion — Morice Square to St Budeaux via South Keyham — had occurred in October 1930. The result of the conversion programme was that only one route — Theatre to Peverell — survived by the late spring of 1939 and the outbreak of war resulted in this being given a stay of execution. At the start of the war, the fleet comprised Nos 142-44/51-66 plus two of the ex-Exeter trams (Nos 2 and

6) and six acquired second-hand from Torquay (Nos 10-15) as well as two works cars all based at Milehouse depot.

As a major naval base, Plymouth was bound to be a target for the Luftwaffe during the war and the city suffered serious damage. The tramway was also to be damaged, particularly following the heavy raids of March 1941. On 29 March 1941, the depot at Milehouse was hit whilst No 153 was destroyed in Basket Street and No 158 damaged. Following the raid, the tramway service was temporarily suspended and, when it was restored, the central terminus was cut back from the Theatre to Old Town Street. During 1942, the fleet was further reduced by the withdrawal of Nos 142-44; the ex-Exeter and ex-Torquay trams; and Nos 156/63/64.

By 1945, the operational tram fleet had been reduced to four vehicles — Nos 154/57/58/65 — and on 29 September 1945 Plymouth became the second system formally to abandon its tramway post-war when No 158, which had had to be repaired earlier in the year, carried the official party to Milehouse depot.

DEPOTS

There was only one depot that survived to final closure on 29 September 1945; this was the main depot and workshops situated at Milehouse. This was originally opened by the Devonport & District Tramways Co Ltd on 26 June 1901 and was taken over by the corporation on 20 October 1915. The depot was extended in both 1927 and 1933. There were six other depots that had served Plymouth. Camel's Head depot was opened on 26 June 1901 by the Devonport & District Tramways Co Ltd; closed two years later, it was used to store trams requiring overhaul until 1927 when it was sold. Compton was opened by Plymouth Corporation as a horse tram depot on 3 April 1893; horse trams remained until 4 April 1901 and then it accommodated electric trams until 10 April 1932. Latterly, it was used solely to accommodate withdrawn trams and those on football specials. Manor Lane depot was opened as a horse tram depot by the Plymouth, Stonehouse & Devonport Tramways Co Ltd on 18 March 1873 and closed in 1900. Market Street was also opened by the Plymouth, Stonehouse & Devonport Tramways Co Ltd, on 18 November 1901, to accommodate electric trams and passed to the corporation on 1 July 1922. The depot closed the following year. Millbay depot was opened by the Plymouth, Devonport & District Tramways Co Ltd on 4 November 1884; this accommodated

Following earlier conversions, Plymouth's sole surviving route was from the Theatre to Peverell; here No 158 — one of the trams built during 1927 and 1928 — stands at the Derry's Clock terminus outside the Theatre prior to heading towards Peverell. *Barry Cross Collection/Online Transport Archive*

horse trams and was taken over by the Plymouth Tramways Co Ltd in 1886 and by the corporation six years later. It was closed on 22 June 1907. Finally, Prince Rock depot was opened by the corporation on 22 September 1899 and was finally closed on 22 February 1936.

CLOSURE

29 September 1945   (Theatre) via Old Town Street to Peverell

FLEET

151

No 151 was an experimental open-top bogie car that was built in Plymouth's own workshops in 1925 on maximum traction bogies supplied by the Malleable Steel

Castings Co (1909) Ltd of Pendleton in Manchester. The bogies were replaced by a Peckham P22 truck in 1930/31. The tram was withdrawn in 1945.

152/54/55/57-62/65/66

Following on from the experimental No 151, Plymouth Corporation constructed a batch of 15 trams — Nos 152-166 — during 1927 and 1928. Again fitted with maximum traction bogies supplied by the Malleable Steel Castings Co (1909) Ltd, all were retrucked using Peckham P22 trucks during 1930 and 1931 with the exception of Nos 156/63/64, which were withdrawn in 1942. No 153 was destroyed by enemy action on 29 March 1941 in Basket Street. No 158 sustained serious damage during the same raid but was repaired and returned to service. All were withdrawn in 1945.

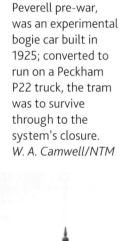

No 151, seen at Peverell pre-war, was an experimental bogie car built in 1925; converted to run on a Peckham P22 truck, the tram was to survive through to the system's closure. *W. A. Camwell/NTM*

A **total** of 10 of the 15 trams built between 1927 and 1928 survived to the end of the system, including No 165 seen here. *F. N. T. Lloyd-Jones/Online Transport Archive*

SEATON

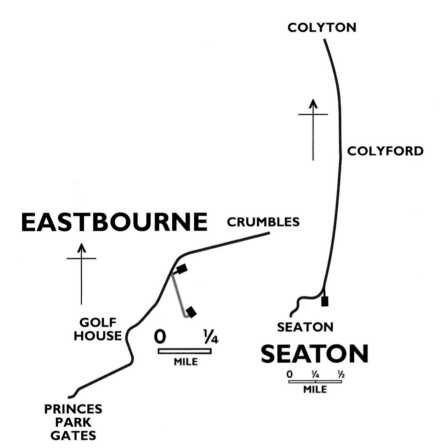

COLYTON

COLYFORD

EASTBOURNE   CRUMBLES

GOLF
HOUSE   0   ¼
MILE

SEATON

SEATON

0   ¼   ½
MILE

PRINCES
PARK
GATES

Born in 1908, Claude Lane was interested in trams from an early age. Following various apprenticeships, he started his first business; this was later followed by the Lancaster Electrical Co Ltd based in Barnet, in Hertfordshire.

After the war, having volunteered as a tram driver at Blackpool and Llandudno, he decided to construct his own tram. This was the 15in-gauge miniature version of one of the ex-Darwen cars sold to the Llandudno & Colwyn Bay Electric Railway, which was completed at the Barnet works

in 1949. To offset the cost on construction, he used the tram at events where it operated over temporary track. This led, in 1951, to its operation for the summer season at St Leonards, on the Sussex coast, and from 1952 to five seasons of summer operation at Rhyl, where the tram was joined by the first of his replica Blackpool trams.

The success of these operations encouraged Lane to negotiate a lease at Eastbourne and establish a new operation there. On 19 May 1953, Modern Electric Tramways Ltd was established and, following the grant of a five-year licence, construction of the 2ft 0in line commenced in March 1954. The first operation — running from the depot westwards to the Golf House (a distance of 230 yards) — commenced on 4 July 1954; the remainder of the initial route, to Princes Park Gates, followed on 15 August 1954. The line operated during the summer months only and reopened the following year at Whitsun.

On 20 April 1956, having failed earlier in the year, Lane obtained permission to extend the line eastwards from the depot to the Crumbles. On 10 October 1956, the concession was extended to the end of the 1963 season. At the end of the year, construction started on the extension as well as the doubling of the section from the depot to the Golf House.

There was, however, a delay in the opening of the Crumbles extension — to May 1958 — as a result of problems with the covenants covering the land over which the tramway was to operate; although

owned by the corporation, Chatsworth Estates, which had gifted the land to the corporation in 1926, had placed restrictions on its use. Following agreement, which included relocating the already laid track, Chatsworth Estates withdrew their objection. This extension was part of Lane's plans — never fulfilled largely due to corporation objections — to see the tramway eventually reach Langney Point.

Towards the end of the 1963 season, the line's lease was renewed for a further year; the same happened at the end of the 1964 season. However, recognising that an annual licence was not an encouragement to invest in the business (particularly as some of the track needed relaying), Lane sought a seven-year licence in

September 1965. However, the corporation was unwilling to agree as the Crumbles was likely to form part of a future development plan including a new road that would cut across the tramway. The plans unveiled in October 1965 effectively meant the necessity of re-siting the entire tramway west of the depot; on 31 October 1967, the corporation served notice on the tramway to relocate the track. In theory, the 1968 season should have been the last at Eastbourne but delays in the project gave the line an additional year; the final trams operated in Eastbourne on 14 September 1969.

A new chapter in the line's history was about to commence; on 24 December 1969, the Transfer Order and Light Railway

The first miniature tram constructed by Claude Lane was a replica of an ex-Darwen streamlined tram and was completed in 1949. Never regauged from 15in, the tram was used on temporary tracks at events and during the summer season at St Leonards. It was eventually to be acquired for preservation. *Phil Tatt/Online Transport Archive*

Eastbourne No
4 was a replica
Blackpool 'Boat'
constructed in 1961;
it is seen at the
somewhat bleak
Crumbles terminus.
Claude Lane had
plans to extend the
tramway further
east to Langney
Point, but he was
to be frustrated in
these ambitions.
*F. E. J. Ward/Online
Transport Archive*

Order for the Seaton branch — which
had closed completely following the
withdrawal of passenger services from
Seaton Junction on 7 March 1966 — meant
that the future lay in Devon.

In February 1970, following the
dismantling of the line, the first
equipment and trams were transferred
to Seaton and work commenced on the
construction of the new line. This was
built to 2ft 9in, resulting in the necessity
of re-gauging of the fleet. Following initial
work, the first services — using No 8
operating on battery power drawn from
a battery wagon towed by the tram —
commenced over the first short section on
28 August 1970.

Work progressed on the extension
to Colyford but, before this could be

completed, Lane died suddenly on 2 April
1971. Work, however, continued and the
line through to Colyford opened — still
using battery power — on 9 April 1971.
Work was progressing on the erection
of overhead; this was first used in
September 1973.

Two extensions followed. The first of
these extended the tramway southwards
from the depot to the entrance of the
Harbour Road car park. Work on this
was started in 1974 with the line formally
opening on 25 May 1975. Work started on
the Colyton extension in November 1975;
work progressed smoothly until 1978,
when floodwater washed away part of
the embankment north of Colyford. The
necessity of additional flood protection
resulted in the opening of the section

Seaton No 7 recorded at the town terminus on 15 September 2004; this was one of the 2ft 0in trams transferred from Eastbourne to Seaton in 1970 and converted to 2ft 9in in 1976. *Author*

through to Colyton — which took the route to just under 3¼ route miles — being delayed until 8 March 1980.

Since the completion of the line, the tramway has undertaken three further significant projects; these are: the opening of a new terminus building in Seaton (completed in 1995); the upgrading and restoration at Colyton station (completed in 1996); and the extension to Riverside depot (officially opened on 28 September 1998).

As passenger traffic has increased — it now averages about 100,000 annually — so the fleet has grown to deal with it. Today, the line remains a popular attraction amongst tourists and birdwatchers, who appreciate the line's value in offering good opportunities for watching the bird life of the Axe Valley. A new town terminus, costing £2 million, was constructed at Seaton over the winter of 2017/18.

DEPOTS
Modern Electric Tramways Ltd established a depot in Eastbourne, located just off Wartling Road at the point where the tramway crossed the access road to the car park before heading east to Crumbles and was linked by a single line to the company's workshop to the south. The depot opened on 4 July 1954 and survived through to the closure of the line on 14 September 1969. It was later demolished. A second depot, located to the south of the original structure, was added in 1960. Following the transfer of operations to Devon, a new Riverside depot was opened at Seaton on 28 August 1970. This depot, extended in 1997, remains in use.

OPENING DATES
Eastbourne:

4 July 1954	Depot to Golf House
15 August 1954	Golf House to Princes Park Gates
May 1958	Depot to Crumbles

Seaton:

28 August 1970	Riverside to Bobsworth Bridge
9 April 1971	Bobsworth Bridge to Colyford
25 May 1975	Riverside to Harbour Road car park
8 March 1980	Colyford to Colyton

CLOSURES
Eastbourne:

14 September 1969	Golf House to Crumbles

FLEET
Prior to the opening of the tramway at Eastbourne, Claude Lane's Lancaster Electrical Co of New Barnet had constructed his first 15in-gauge miniature tram — based upon one of the ex-Darwen English Electric-built streamlined trams of 1936. This was completed in 1949 and used to give children rides. In 1951, the tram was used at St Leonards and, between 1952 and 1956, at Rhyl. This was followed by a replica Blackpool 'Boat' (No 225) and an open-top tram (No 3) that were built to the 15in gauge in 1950 and 1952 respectively. The replica Darwen car was not re-gauged and was eventually preserved, whilst No 3 was converted to 2ft 0in and used at Eastbourne; Nos 3 and 225 were two of three trams sold to the USA in 1963. The final 15in-gauge tram constructed was toastrack No 6, which was completed in 1954 and converted to 2ft 0in on transfer to Eastbourne in 1955 when it was rebuilt as an open-top double-decker. It was further rebuilt in both 1962 and 1990.

Following the opening at Eastbourne, a number of trams were constructed at New Barnet for the line. The first 2ft 0in tram was No 226; this was a further 'Boat' replacement and was to survive until 1960 when it was converted into a works car (No 01) and then in 1965 it was modified to form the tram shop; it was converted in 1995 to form a gangers wagon (again No 01). The next new tram was No 238, which was a replica of a Blackpool 'Balloon' car; this was completed in 1955 and was to be the third tram exported to the USA in 1963. The last tram completed

in the 1950s was No 7; this was an open-top double-deck car completed in 1958. Four trams were added to the fleet during the 1960s; these were: No 4 (a further 'Boat' replica completed in 1961); No 2 (an open-top double-deck car of 1964); No 12 (an enclosed single-deck car of 1966); and No 8 (an open-top double-deck car of 1968). In addition, there was a second works car — No 02 — built at New Barnet originally for, but never used by, the Air Ministry in 1952.

All of the 2ft 0in fleet transferred to Seaton following the closure of the Eastbourne operation. The cars were re-gauged from 2ft 0in to 2ft 9in in 1970 (Nos 2 and 8), 1971 (No 12) and 1976 (Nos 4, 6 and 7). No 8 was rebuilt in 1992 whilst No 12 was rebuilt as an open-top

double-decker in 1980 and again in 1999 when it acquired 'Feltham' style ends.

Since the move to Seaton, a further seven trams have been constructed, all by the company itself, except for the most recent additions. The fleet additions have been as follows (in chronological order): No 14 (this is a single-deck saloon completed in 1984; it was constructed using parts rescued from Metropolitan Electric Tramways No 94 from 1904); No 17 (this is a single-deck crossbench car; completed in 1988, it is designed for wheelchair users); No 16 (this is a single-deck saloon car; completed in 1992, it used the body of Bournemouth Corporation No 106 of 1921); No 19 (completed in 1994 as a single-deck saloon, this reused the rescued body of Exeter Corporation No 19 of 1906); and

Three of the Eastbourne fleet pictured outside the depot. From the left are No 238 (new 1955), No 6 (as rebuilt in 1955) and No 225 (one of the three trams exported to the USA in 1963). Nos 6 and 225 had originally been 15in gauge when built. *Phil Tatt/Online Transport Archive*

A number of the trams built for operation at Eastbourne and then at Seaton have used the parts of older trams; one of these is No 19, which is based upon the body of an ex-Exeter Corporation single-deck tram. No 19 was completed in 1994 and is seen here on 27 July 1998. *Les Folkard/Online Transport Archive*

Nos 9-11 (these three open-top double-deck cars were built by Bolton Trams Ltd between 2002 and 2007).

In addition to the passenger trams, there is also a small fleet of works vehicles. Apart from Nos 01 and 02, these include a welding trailer (No 03), a hydraulic hoist (No 04), a drop-side wagon (No 06) and a diesel tractor (No 06).

SOUTHAMPTON

In the 1930s, the state of the track and the age of the fleet led to a debate about the future of Southampton's tramways. Although the trams had been profitable, little had been done to ensure their future, with the profits being used to support the rates rather than being invested for the future of the tramway. In the mid-1930s, two routes were converted to bus operation: that to Millbrook on 2 October 1935 (although a workmen's service continued thereafter) and the short route from Clock Tower to Northam on 4 June 1936; the latter had not been a success as the existence of a toll bridge had prevented it being linked up to Bitterne.

Following a debate, it was agreed that the trams should be converted by 1940 and that the trolleybus was the preferred alternative mode of transport. Powers to operate trolleybuses were obtained in 1937 but, in the event, were never exercised.

Little had been done to progress the closure programme by the outbreak of war and so the increasingly aged fleet persevered through the hostilities. Although as a port city, Southampton was a major target for the Luftwaffe and was seriously damaged, the trams escaped relatively lightly, although No 31 was destroyed on 30 November 1940 by an incendiary and No 13 was to be damaged. Recognising the threat to the fleet posed by accommodating them in the vulnerable depots at Portswood and Shirley, the corporation built two storage sidings (to the east and west of the Bassett crossroads), to which the trams were dispersed each evening. Thereafter, the

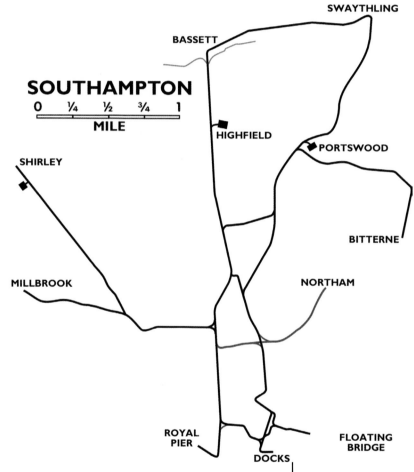

closest the fleet came to further harm was in November 1942 when a child playing on one of the trams accidentally released a brake, causing it and two others to roll away; fortunately, the trio were stopped before serious damage resulted.

As the war drew to a close, the future of the tramway was again under consideration and, in mid-1944, the chairman of the Transport Committee confirmed that the trams were to be replaced as part of the post-war

On 19 May 1946 No 50 was used on an LRTL tour of the Southampton system; it is seen here at the Floating Bridge terminus. There was a short section of horse tramway from here to the Docks terminus that was never electrified. Floating Bridge ceased to be a tram terminus on 31 December 1949 when the last Southampton trams operated. *F. E. J. Ward/Online Transport Archive*

No 87 stands at Royal Pier with a route 1 service to Bassett on 29 June 1946; this service would survive until conversion to bus operation on 5 March 1949. In the background can be seen some of the extensive bomb damage that Southampton suffered during the war. *Ian L. Wright/ Online Transport Archive*

reconstruction of the city. However, in place of the trolleybus, the diesel bus was now to be adopted. As a result of the problems of obtaining replacement buses, it was not until towards the end of the decade that it proved possible to commence the conversion programme.

The first casualty, on 15 May 1948, saw trams withdrawn from the Bitterne Park to Docks via St Mary's route. In August 1948, the LRTL organised a tour of the Southampton system; this was one of a number run during the post-war years, but this one was to be of historical significance. During the course of the tour, participants noticed a number of elderly trams in the process of being scrapped; they decided to raise the funds — £10 — required to purchase one, with No 45 being selected. The successful purchase — which required an appeal in *Modern Tramway* finally to reach its target — resulted in the first tram to be privately preserved in Britain. This was

the start of what became the LRTL's Museum Committee, which morphed eventually into the Tramway Museum Society and the National Tramway Museum.

The next conversion occurred on 30 October 1948, with the demise of the service from Swaythling to Stag Gates via Portswood and Lodge Road; although no longer served by passenger trams, access to Portswood was retained to permit trams to get to and from the depot. The next route conversion saw the route from Swaythling to Avenue Junction via Burgess Road and Bassett replaced by buses on 5 March 1949. About this time (if not earlier) — and there is some uncertainty about the exact date — the workmen's service to Millbrook ceased. The route was certainly still passable until 5 July 1947 and was covered by the LRTL special on 29 August 1948.

The final route — from Floating Bridge to Shirley — was to survive until the end

Southampton's last tram on 31 December 1949 was No 9, which was suitably decorated for the occasion. It is seen here at Junction during the final day. *F. E. J. Ward/Online Transport Archive*

of 1949, with the last trams operating on New Year's Eve. The official last tram was No 9, which operated on the last day suitably decorated before arriving at Shirley depot just before midnight to mark the end of the system.

No 9 was not the last tram, however, to operate over the system; power was retained to permit the transfer of trams from Shirley to Portswood for disposal and the last trams to make the journey were Nos 21 and 101 on 4 February 1950. After closure, a number of trams were sold to Leeds Corporation, although not all entered service and a number of those sold were scrapped in Southampton without making the journey north. Although No 45 was secured for preservation before the system closed, a further three bodies — of Nos 11, 38 and 57 — have been subsequently rescued with restoration of No 11 some 85 per cent complete at the time of writing.

DEPOTS

Southampton Corporation possessed two depots through the electric tramcar era. The older of the two was that at Portswood; this had originally opened on 5 May 1879 as a horse tram depot for the Southampton Tramways Co Ltd. This was taken over by Southampton Corporation on 30 June 1898 and extended considerably two years later to accommodate the new electric trams and to provide workshop facilities; from 1908 onwards, the majority of new trams built for operation by Southampton had bodies constructed at Portswood. The depot ceased to house operational cars on 5 March 1949, but was used to store withdrawn cars into 1950. The second depot, at Shirley, was opened by the Southampton Tramways Co on 9 June 1879. Again acquired by the corporation in 1898, horse trams survived until 21 June 1900 and then it was used by electric trams until the system's final closure on 31 December 1949.

CLOSURES

15 May 1948	Bitterne to Docks via St Mary's
30 October 1948	Swaythling to Stag Gates via Portswood and Lodge Road
5 March 1949	Swaythling to Junction (via Bassett)
31 December 1949	Floating Bridge to Shirley.

FLEET

1-6, 30

Following on from the initial trams delivered in 1899 (see Nos 33/34/36/39, 40), Milnes supplied two batches of trams in 1901. Nos 30-37 were fitted with short canopies; this resulted in an increase in seating on the upper deck for the latter batch to 33 from 28 on Nos 21-29. Nos 30-37 were fitted with Brill 21E trucks. In 1912, Nos 32 and 34 were rebuilt with balcony covers and two years later Nos 30 and 31 were fitted with extended lower-deck canopies. In 1922, Nos 32 and 34 exchanged numbers with Nos 30 and 31 respectively. In 1923, there was a further renumbering, with Nos 32 (ex-30), 33, 34 (ex-31), 35-37 becoming Nos 11, 10, 7, 8, 6 and 9 respectively. Obviously, Southampton enjoyed renumbering its fleet as, in 1925, five of the cars — Nos 7-11 — were renumbered 3, 2, 5, 1 and 4 respectively. In 1929, two cars, Nos 32 (ex-30) and 31 (ex-34) were rebuilt with the Bargate-style roof; the remaining cars were rebuilt the following year. The first of the batch to be withdrawn was No 31, which succumbed in 1940. The remainder survived to be withdrawn in 1945 (No 5) and 1949 (Nos 1-4, 6 and 30). All were scrapped after withdrawal.

7-11

Between 1920 and 1924, five open-top double-deck cars were built at Portswood on Brill 21E cars. These were Nos 2 and 40 (in 1920), Nos 4 and 5 (in 1923) and

No 3 in 1924. No 40 was renumbered 1 in 1923 and 7 two years later. The other four cars were renumbered in 1925, Nos 2-5 became Nos 10, 11, 9 and 8 respectively. At the same time, all five were rebuilt with Bargate-style domed roofs. Nos 7 and 8 were subsequently fitted with replacement Peckham P35 trucks. Nos 8, 9 and 11 were all withdrawn by 1948, whilst Nos 7 and 10 were taken out of service during 1948. Whilst none of the five was preserved on withdrawal, the body of No 11 was discovered in 1977 and subsequently rescued for preservation. Restoration of the car is proceeding and, once completed, will be the only example of a Bargate-roof car to survive.

12

Completed in 1923, No 12 was the first tram to be built from new with the rounded roof profile designed to permit operation through the Bargate. Constructed at Portswood and fitted initially with a Brill 21E truck, No 12 was eventually to be retrucked with a Peckham P35. The tram was to survive in service until 1949 and, although sold to Leeds Corporation, was one of those that never reached the West Riding, being scrapped in Southampton.

14-20/22, 31/37

Following on from the construction of No 12, the first of the fleet to be constructed with the Bargate-style top deck, a further ten cars with the new roof design were

Southampton

No 2 was one of a batch of open-top trams — Nos 30-37 — supplied by Milnes in 1901. All eight were rebuilt as fully enclosed during 1929 and 1930; No 2 was to survive in service until 1949. *J. Pullen*

In 1946
Southampton No 8 is seen at Holy Rood turning into Bernard Street; until 1914 there had been an east to south curve at this junction. No 8 dated originally to 1923 (as No 5) being rebuilt as fully enclosed two years later. It was withdrawn by 1948. *Ian L. Wright/Online Transport Archive*

constructed at Portswood between 1923 and 1929; these were Nos 13-20/22 and 37. All were fitted with Brill 21E trucks initially, with the exception of Nos 22 and 37, which received Peckham P35s from new. With the exception of No 15, all were later to receive Peckham P35 trucks. In 1944, No 13 was renumbered 31, having lost its roof on Shirley Road during a German raid. All were to survive through until 1949 with the exception of No 31, which had been taken out of service by 1948. A number of the cars were sold to Leeds but none actually entered service in the West Riding although No 19 was allocated No 311 by Leeds before being sent to a pig farm at Farsley where it was dismantled. Three others were sent to Farsley without being renumbered; these were Nos 14, 22 and 37 whilst a further three that were sold to Leeds — Nos 16, 17 and 20 —were in fact scrapped in Southampton.

21, 23, 25, 32, 35, 50
These six fully-enclosed trams — the second batch of 'Pullman' cars — were constructed in 1930/31 using bodies built in the corporation's own workshops fitted to Peckham P35 trucks. These were the last new trams to be built for Southampton corporation. The trams were fitted with 8ft 0in-wide, flush-sided, bodies and were originally fitted with air brakes. This equipment was later removed following a runaway car. All six were to survive through to the final closure of the system in 1949 and were sold to Leeds Corporation; No 21 was not allocated a Leeds number and was scrapped unused at Farsley. Nos 23, 25, 32, 35 and 50 became Leeds Nos 300, 299, 298, 297 and 296 respectively. The ex-Southampton cars were destined to have a short life in Leeds, being withdrawn during 1952 and 1953.

The first tram built fully enclosed to the Bargate roof profile was No 12 in 1923; on withdrawal, No 12 was purchased by Leeds Corporation but was not to make the journey to Yorkshire. *F. E. J. Ward/Online Transport Archive*

On 9 March 1946 Southampton No 18 is seen on route 5 at Shirley. This was one of 10 Bargate-roof trams built between 1923 and 1929 that were the last Southampton trams to be fitted with Brill 21E trucks when new. The majority — but No 18 — were sold to Leeds Corporation, but none entered service there. *Ian L. Wright/Online Transport Archive*

24/26/27/29

Also supplied by Milnes in 1901 were Nos 21-29, which were uncanopied open-top cars fitted with Brill 21E trucks. In 1914, Nos 24/26/27/29 were rebuilt with extended canopies, increasing the seating capacity on the upper deck to 32. Whilst the modified quartet were to survive through to 1945, the first of the unmodified cars to be withdrawn was No 25 in 1922. Others followed in 1923 (No 21), 1928 (No 22, which was converted into a welding car, No 105E), 1929 (No 23) and 1930 (No 28). The four remaining cars, which remained open-top throughout their career, were withdrawn in 1948 (Nos 24 and 27) and 1949 (Nos 26 and 29).

33/34/36/39, 40

For the opening of Southampton's electric system, Milnes supplied a batch of 20 open-top trams fitted with Brill 21E trucks. Nos 4, 6 and 7 were rebuilt with lower-deck canopies between 1913 and 1915;

this increased the seating capacity on the upper deck from 24 to 32. These three cars were renumbered 40, 34 and 36 in 1923. Between 1923 and 1925 a further 10 cars — Nos 1, 3, 9-13, 15, 19 and 20 — were also renumbered; they became Nos 21, 39, 37, 33, 32, 16, 35, 39, 50 and 25 respectively. The first of the batch to be withdrawn was No 2 in 1919; this car had been converted into a single-deck toastrack car three years earlier. Between 1923 and 1931 a further 14 of the type were withdrawn, leaving five in service. These were to survive through the war years until 1945 when Nos 33 and 39 were withdrawn. The remaining three, Nos 34, 36 and 40, were all withdrawn in 1948. All were scrapped after withdrawal.

38, 41-45/48/49

In 1902, Hurst Nelson supplied a batch of 12 open-top double-deck cars, No 38-49, that were fitted with Brill 21E trucks. Five cars — Nos 38, 41/42/44/49 — were fitted with lower-deck canopies during

No 21 is pictured outside the depot at Shirley; this tram was one of six supplied during 1930 and 1931 that were the last new trams built by the corporation. All six were sold to Leeds Corporation, but No 21 was not to enter service in Yorkshire. *F. E. J. Ward/Online Transport Archive*

1914 and 1915, which increased the seating capacity on the upper deck by eight. No 45 was rebuilt with a top cover in 1917, but this was removed when the car received lower-deck canopies in 1928. With the exception of the brief period when No 45 carried a top cover, the entire batch operated throughout their career in open-top condition. Four of the type were withdrawn between the two world wars — No 40 in 1919, No 39 in 1922 and Nos 46 and 47 in 1929 — but the remainder survived through the Second World War. All were withdrawn in 1948; it was during an LRTL tour of Southampton, when these withdrawn trams were spotted awaiting the attentions of the scrap men, that participants on the trip decided to purchase one for preservation. Following an appeal, No 45 was secured — the

first tramcar to be preserved privately in Britain — and, after having led a peripatetic existence for some years, was to arrive at Crich, where it remains as part of the National Tramway Museum collection. In the 1970s, the body of No 38 was identified and rescued for preservation; it is now owned by the group restoring No 11 and is a long-term restoration project.

51
No 51 was one of two trams acquired by the corporation during the First World War. It was a balcony-top double-deck car constructed in the corporation's own workshops and fitted with a Brill 21E truck. The car was rebuilt with a Bargate-style top cover in 1929 and was to survive in this condition until withdrawal during 1949.

No 27 was one of four survivors post-war of a batch of nine originally new in 1901. Seen here at Portswood, No 27 was to remain in service until 1948. Note the driver leaning out to change the point. The tram is still in the pre-war livery but without the legend Southampton Corporation Tramways' on the rocker panel. *Hugh Nicol/NTM*

No 39, which was No 15 until renumbered in 1924, was one of five survivors from a batch of 20 supplied by G. F. Milnes & Co for the system's opening. This wartime view — note the white-painted buffer beam — was towards the end of the tram's life; it was one of two of the type withdrawn in 1945. *Barry Cross Collection/Online Transport Archive*

Southampton No 45 is pictured in the workshops at Portswood on 1 June 1946; It became the first tram in Britain saved privately and now forms part of the NTM collection. *Ian L. Wright/Online Transport Archive*

52-73

Between 1908 and 1914, Twenty-two open-top cars entered service. These had corporation-built bodies on Brill 21E trucks. Nos 52-55 were new in 1908; Nos 56-59 in 1909; Nos 60-71 in 1912 and the final two in 1914. All were to survive into 1945 but the first casualty was No 55, which succumbed that year. This was followed in 1947 by No 52. The majority of the cars were withdrawn in 1948, leaving seven — Nos 61, 64-66, 69, 71 and 72 — to operate through into 1949. Whilst none was preserved at the time, the body of No 57 was discovered near Romsey in 1975 and acquired by the City Museum

for restoration backed by the TRAM 57 project. The tram body still survives in a largely unrestored condition based at the Hampshire County Museum store.

74

The second of the cars delivered during the First World War, No 74 was an open-top double-decker constructed at Portswood on a Brill 21E truck. Initially fitted with a front-entrance body, the car was later modified. In 1929 it received a Bargate-style top cover and was later to receive a replacement Peckham P35 truck. Withdrawn in 1949, No 74 was one of the cars acquired by Leeds

On **31** October 1949, No 81 is pictured to the south of the Bargate; by this date the gate itself was no longer used by trams, with all trams diverted either side of the mediaeval structure. This tram was one of two delivered during the First World War and had been rebuilt in 1929. *John Meredith/ Online Transport Archive*

Pictured in the PW yard at Highfield on 30 December 1948, by which date it had been withdrawn, No 58 was one of 22 open-top trams acquired between 1908 and 1914. None were rebuilt and all remained as open top through to withdrawal. The body of sister car No 57 was secured for preservation in 1975. *F. E. J. Ward/Online Transport Archive*

Corporation, but scrapped on the south coast without ever making its way to the West Riding.

76-80

In 1918, Southampton acquired six trams second-hand from the London County Council; Nos 75-80 were originally LCC Nos 193/96-98, 200/01 respectively and had been new in 1903. The cars were built by ERTCW and fitted with Brill 21E trucks. When delivered to Southampton, the cars were fitted with fully-enclosed top decks, but these covers were removed in 1922 to permit operation under the Bargate. Although No 75 was withdrawn in 1934, the remaining five cars survived through to be withdrawn in 1947 (No 77) and 1948 the remainder. All were scrapped on withdrawal.

81

In 1917 and 1918, the corporation constructed two open-balcony four-wheel cars at Portswood on Brill 21E trucks. Both of these were rebuilt with Bargate-profile

fully-enclosed top decks in about 1929, albeit retaining open lower-deck vestibules. Whilst No 51 was withdrawn in the same year that it received a new top cover, No 81 was to survive in service until 1948.

82-87/89-91

The last trams acquired by Southampton from an outside supplier were ten open-balcony cars supplied by English Electric in 1920. Fitted with Brill 21E trucks, all bar No 88, which was withdrawn in 1932, survived into 1945. No 84 was withdrawn that year with Nos 87 and 91 following in 1948. The remaining six cars remained operational until withdrawal in 1949. All were scrapped following withdrawal.

92-103

These 12 cars were fully-enclosed double-deckers that were constructed between 1926 and 1929. Built in the corporation's own workshops, all were fitted with Peckham P35 trucks. All were to survive

During 1946 one of the six open-top trams acquired from the London County Council, No 76, is pictured at the Royal Pier with a service for Bassett. Four of the type — including No 76 — survived through until 1948. *Ian L. Wright/Online Transport Archive*

through to the final year of tramway operation in Southampton and were sold for further service to Leeds. However, none actually entered service in the West Riding although fleet numbers were allocated. Nos 92, 95, 97, 99, 101 and 103 were to become Leeds Nos 304, 302, 306, 303, 307 and 301 respectively but were scrapped without being used. Two others — Nos 100 and 102 — were allocated Leeds numbers (312 and 308 respectively), but were sent to a farm at Farsley where they were dismantled for spares along with two others — Southampton Nos 96 and 98 — that were never allocated fleet numbers by Leeds. The remaining two cars — Nos 93 and 94 — were scrapped in Southampton and never made the trip north.

104-09
Constructed in 1929/30, these six fully-enclosed trams — the first of the 'Pullmans' — had 8ft-wide flush-sided bodies built in the corporation's own workshops fitted to Peckham P35 trucks. All were to survive until withdrawal in mid-1949 and were then sold to Leeds Corporation for further use. Nos 104-09 were renumbered 295, 294, 293, 292, 290 and 291 respectively where they were destined to have a short life being withdrawn during 1952 and 1953.

WORKS TRAMS
Southampton employed four dedicated works trams. Two of these, built in 1911, were open wagons fitted on Brill 21E trucks. The third was a snowplough, No 72, and the fourth a welding car, No 105E, that was rebuilt in 1928 from 1901-built No 22. This had originally been a Milnes-built open-top double-deck tram fitted with a Brill 21E truck.

No 81 was originally new in 1918 as an open-top double-decker; rebuilt with a Bargate-profile top-deck cover in 1929, it was to retain its open lower-deck vestibules through to withdrawal in 1948.
F. E. J. Ward/Online Transport Archive

No 85 is pictured inside the No 3 shed at Shirley depot on 30 December 1948. This was one of 10 trams supplied by English Electric and were the last trams acquired from an outside supplier. They retained open balconies and lower-deck vestibules for their entire operational career. *F. E. J. Ward/Online Transport Archive*

The last day of operation — 31 December 1949 — sees No 98 on Shirley Road; this was one of 12 trams built by the corporation between 1926 and 1929. All were sold to Leeds Corporation but none entered service. No 98 was dismantled by Leeds for spares after its transfer to Yorkshire. *John Meredith/Online Transport Archive*

Numerically the last Southampton passenger car, No 109 is seen on 31 December 1948 on Winn Road with a service for the Royal Pier. On withdrawal, No 109 was sold to Leeds, becoming No 291 in that corporation's fleet. *F. E. J. Ward/Online Transport Archive*

The sett car is pictured at the junction of Park Street and Shirley High Street having come from Shirley depot on 20 April 1949. *F. E. J. Ward/Online Transport Archive*

PRESERVATION

There is a significant number of trams from the region covered in this book that have survived into preservation, although a substantial number of these survive solely as derelict bodies and represent long-term restoration projects.

In terms of those trams, the National Tramway Museum houses Chesterfield Corporation No 8; this was built originally in 1899 and withdrawn in 1904. Acquired and restored by Chesterfield Corporation, it became part of the British Transport Commission collection before passing to Crich. Also in fully restored condition is Wolverhampton Tramways Co No 23; this was built by Falcon of Loughborough in 1892 and was acquired for preservation in 1973. It is currently housed at the Black Country Living Museum at Dudley.

The only surviving Bristol tram is the body of a Bristol Tramways Co horse tram dating to 1895. This is currently part-restored for eventual display in its home city. Also under restoration, this time at the Oxford Bus Museum at Long Hanborough, is a City

The first tram from the area covered in this book to be preserved — indeed one of the first to be preserved anywhere in the British Isles — was Portsmouth No 84; this historically important tram is seen in North End depot on 1 August 1946. *Ian L. Wright/Online Transport Archive*

of Gloucester Tramway Co 1880-built horse tram. Also stored at Long Hanborough are the parts of two of the horse trams that once operated in Oxford. There is also one surviving horse tram from the Cambridge Street Tramways Co; this is No 7, which was built by Starbuck in Birkenhead in 1880, and, following acquisition in 2003, is currently under restoration at the Ipswich Transport Museum.

Finally, there are two horse trams from the Leamington & Warwick Tramways. One of these, No 8 of 1880, is currently undergoing restoration at Beamish; when completed the restored car is to appear as Newcastle & Gosforth No 49. The second survivor is No 1, which was probably built by Brown Marshall of Birmingham in 1881 and is stored in an unrestored condition at the National Tramway Museum.

Survivals from the steam tram era are limited; the only substantial survivor is the

trailer rebuilt by Milton Keynes Museum that once operated on the LNWR-owned Wolverton & Stony Stratford. This was rebuilt from the existing lower deck allied to a new top deck built from the original plans and replica bogies funded by a grant from the Transport Trust. Another unique survivor is the body of one of the cable cars operated by Birmingham Central Tramways; built in 1888, by Falcon of Loughborough, this car is stored at the Black Country Living Museum.

The Black Country Living Museum is also home to a number of electric trams from the region and is capable of operating them on a 3ft 6in gauge route that traverses the site. Three of these have been restored to an operable condition. These are double-deck Wolverhampton Corporation No 49, built by UEC in 1909, single-deck Wolverhampton District No 34, built by the Birmingham & Midland

In August 1972 Lowestoft No 14 is pictured at the East Anglian Transport museum at Carlton Colville. Built to 3ft 6in gauge, the tram's body has been fitted to a standard gauge truck — hence the truck extended beyond the rocker panels of the body. *Michael H. Waller*

Tramways Joint Committee at Tividale in 1919, and Dudley, Stourbridge & District No 5, which was also built at Tividale but in 1920. All three were restored following many years of other use; the body of No 49, for example, being used for a period as a coffin store. In addition, the museum accommodates the bodies of three other trams — Wolverhampton District No 102 (built at Tividale in 1919) and two further Dudley, Stourbridge & District cars (No 75 of 1919 and one of the batch of 16, Nos 23-38, that were built in 1901).

The National Tramway Museum at Crich in Derbyshire possesses one of the largest collections of preserved trams in the world. Amongst its collection are a number from the East Midlands. Three of these are restored, although only one is currently operational. Derby Corporation No 1 was built by Brush in 1901 and was withdrawn in 1933. After some years as a summerhouse, its body was rescued for preservation in 1962. Following restoration in the 1990s it was fitted with a 4ft 8½in truck although it was originally operated on the 4ft 0in gauge. Chesterfield Corporation No 7 was again built by Brush but in 1904; withdrawn in 1927 it was rescued and restored in 1997. Leicester No 76 was built by ERTCW in Preston in 1904; withdrawn in 1947, it was rescued in August 1960 and, in 1969, became the first of the NTM's collection be restored from a near derelict condition. The NTM also owns Southampton No 45 and the parts for three Nottingham trams; these are the lower deck of 1902-built No 92, one lower-deck cab section from 1908-built No 121 and the lower deck of 1920-built No 166.

Part of a fourth ex-Nottingham tram body also survives; this is part of the lower deck of 1902-built No 45 which is stored at Ruddington. A second Leicester tram, No 31 (built by ERTCW in 1904), is currently undergoing restoration in its home city following preservation in 2009.

Recently transferred to the National Tramway Museum is Bournemouth No 85. This was built by UEC in 1914 and was sold to the Llandudno & Colwyn Bay Electric Railway in 1936 as No 6. Withdrawn when the Welsh line closed in 1956, the car was preserved. Displayed as part of the BTC collection at Clapham for some years and later at Christchurch, the car is now restored to its Bournemouth condition.

A third operational museum in the region covered by this volume is the East Anglian Transport Museum at Carlton Colville. Whilst this museum has no operational trams from the region at present, it does have parts from three local cars. Currently under long-term restoration is Lowestoft No 14; this was built in 1904 by Milnes and was withdrawn in 1931. Acquired in 1962, the car now sits on a 4ft 8½in gauge truck in place of the 3ft 6in one that it would have had originally. The museum also possesses the body of a second ex-Lowestoft tram, a single-deck car dating from 1903, and the remains of the only surviving ex-Norwich car — No 39; this was originally built by English Electric in 1924.

To the south of Lowestoft, the Ipswich Transport Museum accommodates the only surviving ex-Ipswich tram. This is No 33, which was built by Brush in 1904 and withdrawn in 1926. Rescued after 50 years in 1976, a ten-year programme to see the car restored was completed in 2012.

The largest individual tramway in this volume was the 3ft 6in gauge system operated by Birmingham Corporation; one Birmingham car — No 395, which was built by UEC at Preston in 1911 — was retained by the corporation when the system closed and is now on display at the city's Millennium Point. The lower saloon of a second car — No 107, a UEC production of 1907 — was rescued in 1988 and is undergoing restoration in Birmingham.

Elsewhere there are two more largely complete cars on static display. The only surviving Portsmouth Corporation tram — No 84 — is on display at Basingstoke. This car was originally a

In **1936** the Llandudno & Colwyn Bay Electric Railway purchased 11 redundant trams from Bournemouth Corporation; following the closure of the line in North Wales, the oldest of the 11 — ex-Bournemouth No 85 — was secured for preservation. It is seen here in the Bournemouth Transport depot on 22 June 1991 having been repainted into Bournemouth Corporation livery. *Author*

Milnes-built horse car supplied to the North Metropolitan Tramways. Sold to Provincial Tramways, Portsmouth, in 1896, it passed to Portsmouth Corporation in 1903 when it was rebuilt as an electric car. Used for a period as a railgrinder, it was preserved in 1936 and restored to 1912 condition in 1961. The second car is Cheltenham & District No 21, which was originally built by English Electric in 1921. After a somewhat peripatetic life after preservation in 1961 and cosmetic restoration, it passed to the ownership of Cheltenham Borough Council in 1992 and awaits a full restoration.

The bodies of three other Bournemouth trams are also awaiting restoration. Two — No 86 (again a product of UEC in 1914) and No 101 (originally built by Brush in 1921) — belong to the Llandudno & Colwyn Bay Tramway Society and the latter's body has been restored to replicate the look of the ex-Bournemouth cars when in operation with the L&CBER. The third, No 13 (built by Milnes in 1902), was rescued from a farm in Shropshire and is now based at the Telford Steam Railway.

Elsewhere there are a number of other bodies in varying states of repair. Two ex-Portsdown & Horndean Light Railway cars survive; No 8 is at the Rural Life Centre at Farnham whilst No 13 is under restoration in Portsmouth. Both were built by BEC in 1903. Further along the coast, the only surviving Brighton car, No 53, built by the corporation in 1937, is undergoing restoration in its home town whilst the bodies of two Hastings cars — Nos 48 and 56 (both built by UEC in 1906) — are under restoration at Robertsbridge. Luton Corporation No 6, a UEC car of 1908, is awaiting restoration in its home town, whilst Maidstone demi-car No 18, built by UEC in 1919, is stored in Dover. The lower deck Swindon Corporation No 13, an English Electric-built car of 1921, is stored in the Forest of Dean and the lower deck of Northampton No 21, built by ERTCW in 1905, is stored at Walton-on-the-Naze. Finally, the Blists

Hill Museum of the Ironbridge Museum Trust displays the body of Birmingham & Midlands Tramways No 12, built by Brush in 1904; this car was converted into a gospel hall when withdrawn and is displayed in this condition.

The Seaton & District Electric Tramway has a number of trams that it has rebuilt from tram bodies from other systems. No 14, which was built in 1984, utilises the body of Metropolitan Electric Tramways No 94, whilst No 16 is based upon Bournemouth No 106. The most significant, however, is perhaps No 19, which was built from the body of an Exeter single-deck car in 1998.

There is one further operational tram that requires mentioning; this is Burton & Ashby No 14. The 3ft 6in gauge tram was new in 1906; its lower deck was rescued for preservation in 1970 and restored using a 3ft 0in gauge truck from Lisbon for operation on a tourist tramway in Detroit, where it was based from 1980 until 2003. After languishing for a number of years it was put up for sale in October 2014. Bought the following month, it was repatriated to the United Kingdom and is currently based at Statfold Barn. It was restored to working order – using battery power and regenerative braking – in March 2017.

The Black Country Museum houses a number of 3ft 6in gauge trams; these include ex-Dudley & Stourbridge 5 seen on 25 April 1987. *Les Folkard/Online Transport archive*

BIBLIOGRAPHY

ANDERSON, R.C., *Tramways of East Anglia*; LRTL; 1969

BETT, W.H. and GILHAM J.C., PRICE, J.H. (ed), *The Tramways of Kent*; LRTL; undated

BETT, W.H. and GILHAM J.C., PRICE, J.H. (ed), *The Tramways of South Yorkshire and Humberside*; LRTL; undated

BETT, W.H. and GILHAM J.C., PRICE, J.H. (ed), *The Tramways of South-West England*; LRTL; undated

BETT, W.H. and GILHAM J.C., PRICE, J.H. (ed), *The Tramways of the East Midlands*; LRTL; undated

BETT, W.H. and GILHAM J.C., PRICE, J.H. (ed), *The Tramways of the South Midlands*; LRTL; undated

BETT, W.H. and GILHAM J.C., WISEMAN, R.J.S. (ed), *The Tramways of the West Midlands*; LRTL. undated

BURROWS, V.E., *The Tramways of Southend-on-Sea*; Advertiser Press; 1965

COLLINS, Paul, *Ian Allan Transport Library: Birmingham Corporation Transport 1939-1969*; Ian Allan Publishing; 1999

COLLINS, Paul, *Ian Allan Transport Library: Birmingham Corporation Transport 1904-1939*; Ian Allan Publishing; 1999

CREESE, Geoff, *Leicester and its Trams*; Irwell Press; 2006

CREESE, Geoff, *Leicester's Trams*; Irwell Press; 2000

DAVEY, Peter, *Bristol Tramways*; Middleton Press; 1995

GENTRY, P.W., *The Tramways of the West of England*; author and C.S.N. Walker; 1952

GILHAM, J.C., WISEMAN, R.J.S. (ed), *The Tramways of the South Coast*; LRTL undated

HARLEY, Robert J., *Maidstone and Chatham Tramways*; Middleton Press; 1994

HORNE, John B., *100 Years of Southampton Transport*; Southampton City Transport/ Southampton City Museums; 1979

LAWSON, P.W. *Birmingham Corporation Tramway Rolling Stock*; Birmingham Transport Historical Group; 1983

MACKLEY, David, *Norwich Tramways*; Middleton Press; 2000

MAYOU, Archie, BARKER, Terry and STANFORD, John, *Birmingham Corporation Tramways: Trams and Trolleybuses*; TPC; 1982

Modern Tramway/Tramways & Urban Transit; Light Railway Transport League; 1937 onwards

PROUDLOCK, Noel, *Leeds: A History of its Tramways*; published by the author; 1991

SAMBOURNE, R.C., *Plymouth: 100 Years of Street Travel*; Glasney Press; undated

Tramway Review; Light Railway Transport League; 1950 onwards

TURNER, Keith, SMITH, Shirley and SMITH, Paul: *The Directory of British Tramway Depots*; OPC; 2001

WALLER, Michael H. and WALLER, Peter: *British & Irish Tramway Systems since 1945*; Ian Allan Ltd; 1992

WALLER, Peter: *The Classic Trams*; Ian Allan Ltd; 1993